R 3-00

COOKING
CRYSTAL
CRAFT

BEATRICE HELLER

COOKING CRYSTAL CRAFT

CHILTON BOOK COMPANY RADNOR, PENNSYLVANIA

Copyright © 1975 by Beatrice Heller
First Edition   All Rights Reserved
Published in Radnor, Pa., by Chilton Book Company
and simultaneously in Don Mills, Ontario, Canada,
by Thomas Nelson & Sons, Ltd.
Manufactured in the United States of America

Library of Congress Cataloging in Publication Data

Heller, Beatrice.
     Cooking crystal craft.

     (Chilton's creative crafts series)
     Includes index.
     1. Plastics craft. I. Title.
TT297.H44   745.57   75-4248
ISBN 0-8019-6181-5
ISBN 0-8019-6182-3 pbk.

Cooking crystals making up the background of the
     jacket are courtesy of Quincrafts Corporation.
Projects pictured on the jacket are by the author.
Photographs by Karl Leopold Metzenberg
Drawings by Judy O'Rourke

CONTENTS

LIST OF ILLUSTRATIONS

LIST OF COLOR ILLUSTRATIONS

COOKING
CRYSTAL
CRAFT

CHAPTER 1

Introduction to Cooking Crystal Craft

WHEN people reminisce about the '60s, they will, of course, speak of moon shots, cold wars, riots, assassinations, the Beatles, Flower Children, etc. Eventually someone will recall Dustin Hoffman and *The Graduate*, for the whispered word "Plastics!" may very well become the classic piece of advice to a young man about to launch a career. It was sometime during this decade, you see, that the potato salad you carried home from the market lost its paper container and gained its plastic one; the magic word was, indeed, "plastics."

The raw plastic used to make these containers looks like large granules of sugar. They melt at a temperature of 350° and fuse into any predetermined shape. The granules are known in the plastic and petroleum industries as polystyrene or polystyrene resin. They are manufactured by such giants in the petroleum and chemical industries as Shell, Dow Chemical, and Monsanto. Industry, of course, uses extruding and vacuum forming methods, as well as injection, compression, and blow molding devices, to fabricate not only containers, but toys, housewares, and appliance parts.

WHAT ARE COOKING CRYSTALS?

The craft and hobby industry, always alert for new and interesting materials, saw the potential of these polystyrene granules. Why wouldn't they melt and fuse in an ordinary 350° kitchen oven? Why not use them to create all types of ornaments and useful items: inexpensive, virtually unbreakable, and resembling fine stained glass? And so, cooking crystals were born.

In the early '60s, working with cooking crystals was not always a joyful and satisfying experience. One of the problems was color. Most of the

1

hobby manufacturing companies packaged only clear, transparent crystals. They recommended coloring them yourself with powdered dyes that were sold separately. This meant that you put a cup of crystals together with a teaspoonful of dye in a covered container and shook vigorously to coat each granule. The results were patchy, pastel colors that were impossible to match if you hadn't mixed enough. It also caused uneven blotches of coloring in the finished product where the dye was visible as a darker ring around each melted granule.

Another problem was the inconsistency in the quality and size of the granules sold. They ranged from powdered, through finely ground, to coarse. Although the finished product looked the same regardless of granule size, the length of time needed to bake the piece varied. You could never say to yourself with absolute assurance, "I'll bake this piece for 10 to 20 minutes." If the granules were fine, it might take 5 minutes; if coarse, 40. Although no great harm was done, you never felt you were mastering the craft.

Yet, in spite of the frustrations, it was a craft that appealed to a lot of people. You could bring to it whatever creative ability you had. Whether you were a child of three filling a tart mold or an artistic adult making a three-dimensional floral arrangement, you had the same sense of pride when the finished product was removed from the oven in only a matter of minutes.

So cooking crystal craft enjoyed a span of popularity that lasted perhaps four or five years. People who are interested in hobbies, crafts, and do-it-yourself projects know that there are always several crafts that are "in" at any given moment. Do you have more needlepoint pillows than you need? Did you macrame more belts than you could wear? Make more candles than you could burn? More decoupaged boxes than you have things to put in them?

Yet, for various individual reasons, some crafts will retain their appeal for you longer than others. In spite of their current state of "in-or-outness," you continue to work with them. They seem to evoke more of your creative ability and every project completed leads to another new idea—something else you want to try or another refinement to a process you just discovered. Well, cooking crystals were out, but the few devotees who continued to work in this medium knew of the continued improvements in color and quality.

Cooking crystals are now available in at least a dozen brilliant transparent colors, in addition to three opaque ones which are used as accents. The colors are extruded with the granules so that there is no blotchiness. The granules are large and easy to work with. And now preformed metal frames are available in nearly all hobby or craft shops, substantially simplifying the craft and contributing to its revival. Happily, cooking crystals are "in" again.

The purpose and scope of this book are a clear and detailed presentation of basics for the beginner and a review of all the new techniques, including advances made by people who have never given up on the craft. If you've never worked with this material before, this book will tell you how; if you're familiar with cooking crystals, this book will give you new ideas and show you new avenues to follow.

CHARACTERISTICS OF COOKING CRYSTALS

To begin at the beginning, then, cooking crystals are small, usually transparent pellets of thermoplastic which melt in a kitchen oven (or electric frying pan or toaster oven) at 350°. They are generally sold in prepackaged 5–8 ounce containers with a choice of 10 or 15 colors. If the crystals you buy come in plastic bags, you will find tie twists convenient and necessary closures. Better still, you might want to transfer the crystals to wide-mouthed glass or plastic jars. These are more convenient for both working use and storage.

As the crystals melt, they enter a viscous, gummy stage, causing each granule to blend and fuse with all the surrounding granules. If melted in a mold, the granules take on the exact shape of the mold. On a flat surface, such as a cookie sheet or a piece of aluminum foil, the melting granules do not run or spread, but fuse in the same shape in which you placed them. For this reason, it is important to spread the crystals as levelly as you can. Otherwise, the thickness of the finished piece will vary.

No additives are required, needed, or wanted. Cooking crystals are not the same as liquid resin; they are a complete product in themselves.

BAKING AND COOLING METHODS

Depending on the overall depth and size of the object being made, baking time can vary from five minutes to an hour. A slight chemical odor is released during the baking process. This odor is neither harmful nor offensive to most people, but adequate ventilation is suggested for those who are more sensitive.

As the granules heat, their appearance changes. If you have an oven with a glass window, you can watch the transformation. If not, the process is not harmed in any way by opening the oven door to peek. At first, the heating granules shimmer, then the surface looks rippled, and finally it becomes smooth and glass-like. If crystals are left in the oven too long, pits and craters appear. It is difficult to leave the cooking crystals in the oven so long that they burn, but eventually the product will turn brown.

Caution. Never put the crystals in an oven over 450°, under broiler heat, or over a gas flame. The crystals will flame and burn under intense heat.

After your project has baked the proper length of time, the mold or foil—along with the cookie sheet or cake pan—is removed from the oven to cool. At this point, and for about a minute thereafter, the *hot* plastic is tacky to the touch and is pliable. For certain projects (which we will discuss later), you will use this minute of pliability to mold, bend, embed, or score the plastic. For most purposes, you will want to make sure that your project cools on a flat surface; if the surface is irregular, the cooling resin may droop or conform to whatever shape it is resting on.

After the first minute of cooling, the hardening process prevents any further shaping or molding. The plastic is by no means cool at this point, but it is brittle. Generally, 15 to 30 minutes are required for a finished piece to be thoroughly cooled. During this time, you will hear cracking and popping noises as the cooling plastic retracts and shrinks from a metal mold. This is entirely normal and is no cause for concern. No harm is being done to the plastic. Cooling can be hastened by placing the plastic alone or in a preformed metal frame under cool, running water. But cool water on a hot metal mold or pan will cause the metal to warp. If you can lift the plastic piece off the pan, it is then okay to hold the plastic under water.

FINISHING METHODS

Aluminum foil will easily peel off a finished piece. A metal mold should release a cooled piece when it is turned upside down. It is always best to begin with a perfectly clean mold, as one that isn't can be stubborn about releasing a piece. If this should happen, merely rap the mold sharply against the edge of the kitchen counter or throw the mold on the floor. The hardened plastic is sturdy enough to withstand such treatment without breaking, but you may dent the metal.

A finished piece of plastic can be returned to the oven where it will revert to the gummy stage. This is often done to add additional granules, and therefore depth, to a piece that has shrunk in baking; to bend a finished piece into a different shape; to eliminate rough edges that might have "crept" up the sides of a mold; or to fuse several pieces together.

Hardened or finished pieces can be drilled, sanded, glued or filed. Some of your projects will be sun catchers for hanging, some you'll want to frame, and many are utilitarian as well as decorative in nature.

TOOLS AND SUPPLIES

Only the simplest equipment is necessary for most of the projects in this book, and you will probably find most of these items around your home or garage.

Hot Mitts and Work Gloves. You will need a pair of sturdy, well insulated *hot mitts* for handling hot pans, and heavy *cotton work or garden gloves* for shaping and manipulating hot, pliable plastic.

Cookie Sheet. A standard *cookie sheet or cake pan* will serve as an adequate oven tray for smaller, ornamental projects. Whenever a particular size or type of pan is necessary, I will specify this in the project's equipment listing.

Pliers. A pair of lightweight household *pliers* will be invaluable to you for many of the projects.

Aluminum Foil. You'll need an ample quantity of regular weight *aluminum foil:* with a few exceptions, you will always line your baking pan with foil before arranging the crystals, because the granules have a tendency to "clean" your pans—any rust or baked-on spots permanently adhere to the plastic piece. You may use quilted foil if you specifically want the crosshatches to appear in the finished design.

Skewer. Holes for hanging finished pieces can be made by heating a *skewer, metal knitting needle, nail, or ice pick* over an open flame and piercing the plastic.

Suction Cups. Although you may simply hang any ornament from a hook or nail, you may wish to use little suction cups that have knobs on them. Transparent ones are particularly good for use on windows.

Cord. You will want cord or thread to hang your finished baubles or ornaments as sun catchers. I recommend thin plastic fishing line, as it is extremely strong and, being transparent, nearly invisible.

Miscellaneous Items. You will need an adequate supply of *old newspapers* on hand; they make clean up much easier and prevent scratches or marring on your work surface. *Tweezers and a small soft-bristled brush* (a paintbrush is fine) will be invaluable aids for eliminating stray granules and evening up your crystals along the borders. You'll also need an ordinary teaspoon or tiny plastic scoop for filling in the patterns with crystals.

SUPPLIERS

Specific tools, equipment, or materials will sometimes be required for a particular project. These will be described in detail when the new technique is introduced. Almost all the supplies you need for this craft are easy to find in any well stocked hobby, craft, or hardware store if you do not already have them. Naturally, whenever you have similar or substitute equipment for the optimal item suggested, you should use it.

However, in the event that you have difficulty finding any particular items, the Sources of Supply listing at the back of the book includes company names and addresses for ordering supplies used in various projects. These are listed by generic category, not brand name. When a specific manufacturer's product is especially applicable or is the only one suitable for a project, the brand name will be listed with the supplier. However, in most instances the particular brand is of no significance, and you can order materials from any supplier listed under "Soldering equipment" or "Jewelry findings."

STARTING YOUR PROJECTS

You will become familiar with cooking crystals and their properties by using them. At this point, you know enough of the basic concepts to follow the instructions for almost any project in this book. Each new technique is discussed in detail when it is first introduced: subsequent projects will utilize these methods. As you move from project to project and chapter to chapter, you will "build" your skills. It is important, therefore, even if you do not actually make every project, to skim through the instructions for each new method before you begin a project.

Above all, however, you should remember that the information and instructions are intended to be used as guidelines. They do not have to be followed exactly, but can be the base upon which you make use of your own creative talents. Don't be afraid to change and adapt any of the instructions to your own needs; make each project uniquely yours!

All of the instructions and information are presented in good faith. Since I can't be with you to oversee their application, however, I can't guarantee complete and absolute satisfaction on every project.

2

Delightful Sun Catchers and Ornaments

YOUR imagination plus cooking crystals can create an endless variety of ornaments, some airily delicate, some fetchingly gaudy. Use preformed metal or bamboo frames, add your own touches to metal frames with additional lead strips, form your own lead outlines from scratch, or make freehand shapes with no frame at all! You'll produce professional finished projects with a personal creative touch that makes these ornaments an ideal gift—if you can bear to part with your labor of love!

This chapter will give you instructions for one project of each type. Of course, you are not restricted to making the item I selected, but you will need to adjust the amount and colors of the materials listed if you choose a different design. For instance, the instructions for making the apple from a preformed mold will serve just as well if you'd rather make a banana; simply adjust the quantity of crystals you use if there is a substantial difference in the size of the frame.

USING PREFORMED METAL FRAMES

Without question, the current revival of interest in cooking crystals can be credited to the introduction of preformed metal shapes. These are small outline forms, similar in concept to coloring book line drawings. A sample assortment of these frames is shown in Figure 2–1; you can obtain them at any craft or hobby shop.

You place the metal shape on a baking pan lined with foil and fill in or "color" the spaces with crystal granules. The frame is not a mold that can be reused; the molten plastic adheres permanently to the frame. Your finished piece will strongly resemble leaded stained glass and these sun catchers are absolutely beautiful hanging in a window.

Fig. 2-1

A sample assortment of preformed metal shapes.

Using these frames is the simplest type of project we will discuss and the professional looking results make a rewarding first project.

Brand names you are likely to find in your local craft store are Bake-a-Craft®, EZE-FORM®, Frame-Ups®, Bake 'ems®, or Stained Crystal Ornament Kit®. Regardless of the brand, you are most likely to find an assortment that includes animals, fruit, flowers, toys, Christmas and religious decorations, zodiac signs, and popular cartoon characters, for about $1 each. The frames are sold singly or in kits that include a frame and packages of cooking crystals in three or four colors. The kits range in price from $2 to $5 and are a convenient way to try the medium without any further commitment to it.

If you are unable to find frames at your local craft or hobby shop, refer to the Sources of Supply listing at the back of the book.

Fig. 2-2

The finished apple, made in
a preformed frame.

TANTALIZING APPLE

For a delightful decorative item that literally looks good enough to eat—or an apple for your teacher—nothing can surpass this glittering red apple (Fig. 2–2).

MATERIALS	EQUIPMENT
4″ diameter apple frame	cookie sheet
small amounts of cooking crystals in red, yellow, green, and brown	aluminum foil, 9″ x 12″
	spoon
	tweezers & brush
cord, string, or thread	hot mitts
suction cup (optional)	newspapers

1. Cover your table or work area with a layer of newspapers to make clean-up easier. Place a smooth piece of aluminum foil, *shiny side up,* on the cookie sheet. The foil must always be larger than the frame so that melting crystal cannot seep to the foil's edge, as the foil will become trapped in the plastic and mar your finished project.

2. Notice that the bottom of the metal frame is flat, and the frame tapers to a fine edge at the top. The tapered metal is specifically designed to prevent gaps from forming as the crystal melts and adheres to the walls of the frame. Make sure the frame is completely flat so that no melting granules can "creep" out of the bottom. The frames are pliable enough to bend. Center the frame on the piece of aluminum foil with the bottom side down.

Fig. 2-3

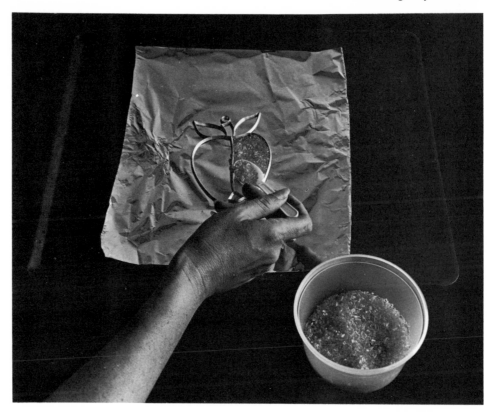

Spooning the crystal granules into the frame (*apple mold by Quincrafts Corp.*).

Fig. 2-4

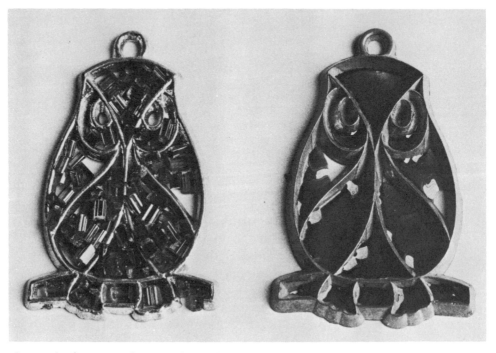

The result of using too few granules (*left*) is producing unwanted gaps in the baked form.

3. Work with one color of crystal at a time. Spoon the granules from the container directly into each section of the frame as shown in Figure 2–3. Fill each area completely so that the bottom surface is entirely covered and the crystals are piled up to a thickness of about ⅛ inch.

The volume of crystals shrinks as the air spaces between them disappear in the melting process. To avoid unwanted gaps in the finished product, you must make sure that you have used enough crystals (Fig. 2–4). Happily, you can add more crystals even after the baking if these gaps do appear. Fill the spaces and return the frame to the oven a second time. The new crystals will melt and blend with the first layer with almost no signs of patching.

Do not put any granules into the little hole at the top of the frame. This space is provided for your string, thread, or cord—which is tied on after the finished frame is removed from the oven.

Stray granules of the wrong color which fall into any section should be removed with tweezers (Fig. 2–5). If allowed to remain, these little spots of

Fig. 2-5

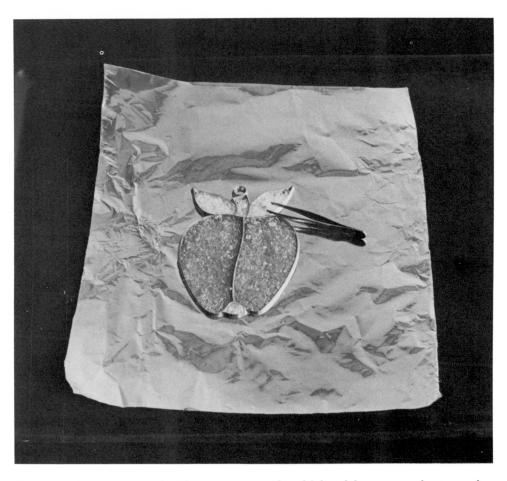

Stray granules are removed with tweezers, avoiding blobs of the wrong color in another compartment.

color are visible and spoil the appearance of your finished work. Brush any stray granules away from the outer edges of the frame, as these would melt and adhere to the frame also. If this should happen, you can file or sand away the excess plastic from the edges of the finished product.

4. Carefully place the pan with the frame on it into an oven preheated to 350°. Bake for 15 minutes before checking its progress. If the plastic has ripples on its surface, leave it in the oven until the surface looks smooth and glass-like—perhaps another 5 minutes.

Remove the pan to a trivet and allow 15 to 20 minutes for cooling.

5. When the apple is cool enough to handle, peel the aluminum foil away from the back.

Fig. 2-6

Transparent cord (fishing line) is tied through the hole at the top of the frame.

Fig. 2-7

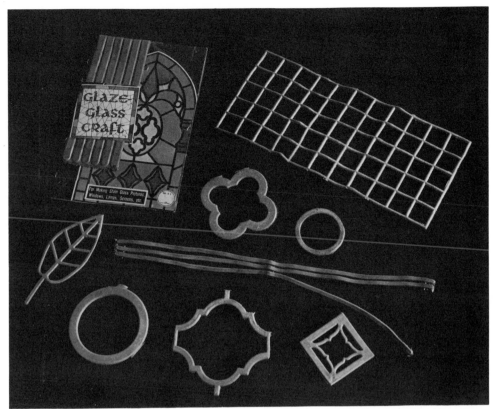

Preformed lead shapes and strips (*Glaze Glass Craft kit by Beagle Manufacturing Co.*).

Tie a length of nylon line or cord through the hole at the top of the apple (Fig. 2–6). Tie the other end of the cord to any hook or nail which enables the finished project to hang freely.

Instead of a hook or nail, you can use the little transparent suction cups that I mentioned in Chapter 1, Tools and Supplies. Both the window and the suction cup should be squeaky clean. Put the cup in place by first bending the sides outward with both hands so that all the air can escape. Don't just press the cup flat into place with one hand as it is more likely to pop off.

Because of the brilliant colors and transparent nature of the finished plastic, these pieces look most attractive with light coming from behind them—either in a window or near a lamp. These decorations are permanent and durable: the colors will not fade, the plastic will not separate from the frame, and the piece is not likely to break if accidentally dropped.

USING PREFORMED LEAD SHAPES AND STRIPS

Anyone who has an aquarium knows about the translucent glass paints used to stain the rear panel. These same paints, without the crystallizing agent, are used by hobbyists to simplify and modernize the craft of leaded stained glass. Instead of cutting separate pieces of glass, molding the lead cames around them, and soldering the pieces together, one can merely glue flat lead strips directly onto a pane of glass and then paint in the colors with glass stain to make very adequate facsimiles.

What could be more logical—or more fun—than to borrow from this craft and further simplify it by using cooking crystals instead of glass stain? The soft, preformed, flat lead strips and shapes are perfect for our needs, but we won't be using glass stain or panes of glass.

Lead Strips. All of the lead shapes and strips are packaged and sold under the name Glaze-Glass Craft® and range in price from 50 cents to $2 (see Sources of Supply). The strips are available in 12-inch lengths in 3 widths: $3/16$ inch for details; ¼ inch for accents; ⅜ inch for outside borders. Traditional background and border shapes available are: 2-, 3- and 4-inch circles; 2- and 3¼-inch rosettes; 1¾- and 3½-inch tiles; and 2- and 3-inch squares. Packages of stylized leaves, a grid of ⅞-inch squares, and a 15-inch butterfly are also available. I have selected the butterfly for our sample project; an assortment of these shapes is shown in Figure 2–7.

Kits are also available which include a pattern for a beautiful stained glass window with all the lead strips and shapes needed. You can use these

Fig. 2–8

Self-adhesive flexible strips (*manufactured by Pactra Industries*).

with cooking crystals, too, but almost all of them are too big to fit into your kitchen oven. You're pretty much limited in size to 14 by 19 inches, which is the largest cookie sheet I've been able to find. So if you're thinking about buying any of these patterns (they are fairly expensive), you'll have to either work in smaller sections and then solder them together or try to modify the pattern size without spoiling the design of the preformed shapes.

You might also want to try a project using Flexi-Lead®, a pliable, rubbery material that resembles lead came. Each package contains a total of 310 inches of Flexi-Lead, in 8-inch strips of 1/8- and 1/12-inch width (Fig. 2–8). Costing approximately $1, the package includes an adhesive called Anchor Film® which makes it possible to apply the strips directly onto the surface of baked crystal pieces. The Anchor Film is sandwiched between two chemically treated papers and has adhesive on both sides. The paper is peeled off one side and applied to the back of the Flexi-Lead. The "lead" strips are then cut or separated with scissors or an X-acto® knife and placed in position on the surface of the hardened plastic. Then the second layer of paper is peeled off and the adhesive remains on the surface of the Flexi-Lead.

If you work with any of these preformed lead shapes or strips, remember to disregard all the instructions that do not apply to the lead shapes. You will not be working with glass or glass stain.

Soldering Iron. You will need an *electric soldering iron.* If you already have one at home, by all means use that one. A note of caution, however: if you use a high wattage iron or soldering gun, solder may

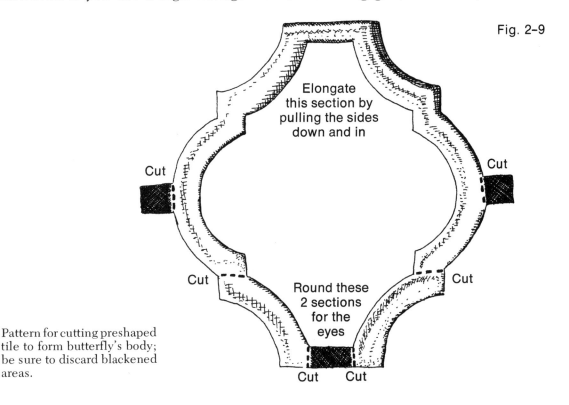

Fig. 2–9

Elongate this section by pulling the sides down and in

Cut

Cut

Cut

Cut

Round these 2 sections for the eyes

Cut   Cut

Pattern for cutting preshaped tile to form butterfly's body; be sure to discard blackened areas.

splatter on your hands or face and you must be extremely careful not to solder right through the lead strips.

If you must purchase an iron, select an 80- or 100-watt soldering iron with an ironclad ⅜-inch tip. A stand to rest the iron on should come with it; if not, use an aluminum pie plate or a piece of asbestos. *Train yourself to use the stand* even when the iron is cold: this simple safety measure will preclude burnt fingers and ruined projects from a rolling hot iron.

Solder. A spool of *resinous core solder* is best for working with crystals. The ratio of tin to lead that you need is 60/40, and you must specify this when you buy the solder. The resinous core is a flux which improves the adherence of the solder to the lead joints.

FLUTTERBY BUTTERFLY

The completed butterfly is shown in the color section, Figure 1.

MATERIALS	EQUIPMENT
15″ lead butterfly shape	cookie sheet
2″ lead circle	aluminum foil
3½″ lead tile	pliers
3/16″ wide lead strip, 12″ long	soldering iron
8 oz. each of cooking crystals in	60/40 resinous core solder
yellow, red, orange, green,	metal skewer
purple	tweezers and brush
cord	scissors
clear acrylic spray (optional)	spoon
	hot mitts
	newspapers

1. Cover the cookie sheet with *one* length of aluminum foil. If two sheets of foil were overlapped, the melting plastic would pick up the overlap as an unwanted seam—and might even embed the edge of the top layer of foil so that you could not remove it later!

I prefer the dull or oxidized look of the lead. However, if you'd like to eliminate the oxidation, clean your butterfly shape and other pieces of lead with vinegar, rinse them with clear water, and then dry them with paper towels before baking the project.

2. With pliers, gently bend and stretch the 2-inch circle into an elongated oval for the butterfly's body. Cut the lead tile as shown in Figure 2–9 and bend the pieces into the proper shapes for the balance of the body and the eyes. Cut the lead strip into two 6-inch lengths and curve them as shown for the antennae.

3. Place the parts of the body and the antennae on the foil, with a wing on either side of the body. Make sure all the pieces lay absolutely flat against the surface of the cookie sheet. All pieces should be placed as closely together as possible.

4. Join both body sections to each wing, using an electric soldering iron and solder. When you touch the end of the solder to the hot soldering iron, a drop of solder melts off much as a droplet of wax would fall off a

Fig. 2-10

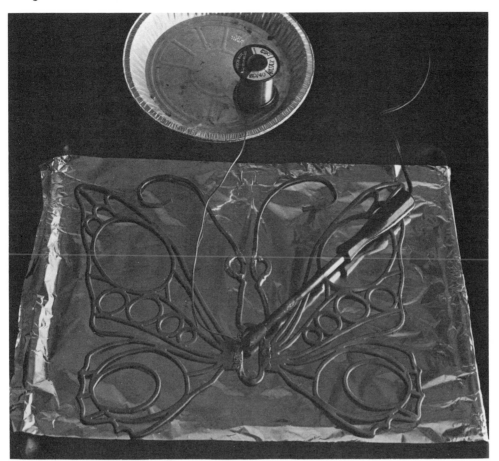

Proximity of solder and soldering iron to the joint; never set a hot iron anywhere except on its stand.

candle. Hold the solder directly on the spot where the pieces are to be joined and then touch with the soldering iron. The solder, when cooled, solidifies and holds the pieces together permanently. Solder *all* sections of the body and the wings together to eliminate any gaps between the pieces of lead.

When you're baking the project, the solder may look as though it's turning to liquid again, but the melting crystal helps keep the pieces together and the solder will resolidify after removal from the oven. The joints are not weakened in any way by this process.

5. Spoon the crystals into each section of the butterfly's wings and body. You may use the color scheme suggested in Figure 2–11 or make your own choice. Make sure each area is fully packed with the granules, but try to keep them off the lead outline as much as possible to keep the lead looking clean. Use your brush to sweep the lead free of crystals.

6. Bake the butterfly on the cookie sheet in a preheated 350° oven for 30 minutes. Check its progress; continue baking if necessary to achieve a smooth, glossy appearance. Remove the cookie sheet from the oven.

Check that all spaces are completely filled. If any gaps are visible, add more crystals and return the piece to the oven. When it is finished, allow it

Fig. 2-11

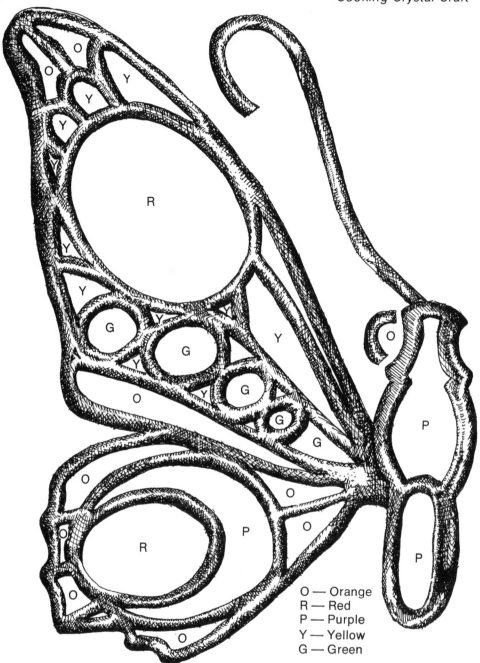

O — Orange
R — Red
P — Purple
Y — Yellow
G — Green

Suggested color combination for the butterfly.

to cool for 20 to 30 minutes before handling it. If you want to retain the shiny silver color permanently, spray with clear acrylic when it has cooled.

7. Because of the weight of the wing span, the butterfly should be hung from a loop attached to both wings rather than from a single point on the body. Using a hot mitt, hold the point of the metal skewer, metal knitting needle, or ice pick in a gas flame until the point is hot (Fig. 2–12).

Fig. 2-12

Be sure to wear a hot mitt when heating your skewer over an open flame.

Fig. 2-13

Piercing the plastic with a hot skewer.

Quickly penetrate the cooled, hardened crystal on both wings as shown in Figure 2–13.

Thread a length of nylon fishing cord through the 2 holes and tie the ends on the back side of the butterfly. Or buy a yard of fine chain at the hobby store. Thread the chain through both holes and, with the pliers, join the end links of the chain together so that the chain becomes one continuous loop.

Now hang the butterfly in a window or anyplace where artificial light can come from behind it.

MAKING YOUR OWN LEAD FRAMES

If you work with lead strips (*cames*) and solder, there is almost no limit to the projects you can make. The designs should be fairly large and simple. You can design your own or borrow ideas from stained glass pieces. An excellent source of patterns is the coloring books used by very young children. You will find large outline drawings of animals, toys, food, and common household objects with wide appeal.

Earlier in this chapter, under "Using Preformed Lead Shapes and Strips" you will find a discussion of the soldering iron and type of solder you'll need. Additional supplies are discussed below.

Lead Cames. You will need to buy both H-shaped and U-shaped lead cames (Fig. 2–14). These usually come in six-foot lengths and cost about $1 each. The U shapes, with a single channel, are used for all outer edges. The channeled edge holds your crystals firmly in place, and the unchanneled edge gives your project a smooth border.

H-shaped cames have a channel on either side and are used for dividing all sections within the body of the project. The wall in the center of a came is a barrier between the channels and also provides it with its H shape. The cames can be molded to shape by hand or with pliers without snapping, if you work firmly but gently.

Fig. 2–14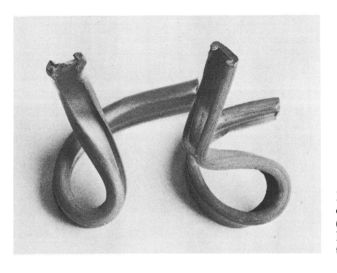

H-shaped and U-shaped lead cames. Note that the U came (*right*) was cut smoothly, leaving a clean edge, while the H came was crushed.

Cames are primarily manufactured for stained glass work, and to that purpose are given standard measurements corresponding to the width of the top surface. For working with cooking crystals, we are concerned with the depth of the inner walls. Crystals require cames with inner walls measuring ⅛ inch in depth; these lead strips are soft and pliable, but walls with deeper channels will buckle when curved. Since *channel depth* will not be specified on the product, I suggest that you carry a ruler along on your shopping trip. If you order by mail, specify your requirements.

Although I have never heard of anyone contracting lead poisoning as a result of handling cames, it pays to take precautions. Wash your hands thoroughly after handling the lead; don't eat while you're working with it; cover any scratches or sores with a bandage before you start.

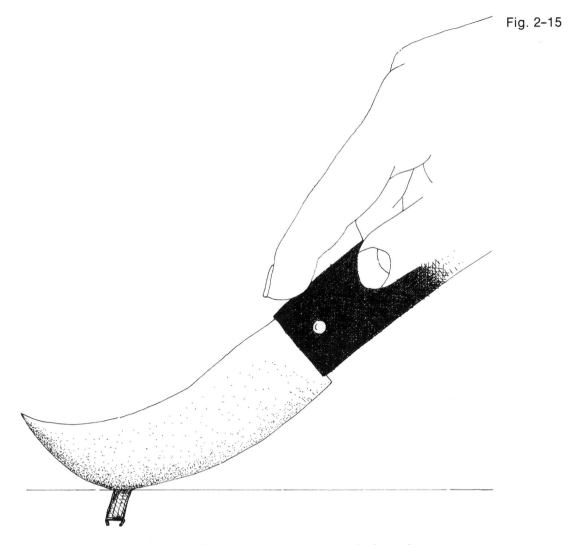

Fig. 2-15

Cutting the lead with a gentle rocking motion so as not to crush the ends.

Caution: Be certain that both the raw materials and the finished products are beyond the reach of infants, small children, or animals who might be inclined to play with them or put them in their mouths.

Lead Cutter. Cames can be cut to the proper length with ordinary scissors or tin snips, but these will tend to crush the ends and cause you difficulty when soldering. This can cause unsightly joints, and the crystal granules may not have enough space in the channels. It is much better to use a lead cutter if you plan to work extensively with cames and are willing to invest in one. If you cannot afford to purchase a lead cutter, a good alternative is a linoleum knife at about one-ninth the cost. The two are similar in appearance because of the curved blade: however, the inner curve of the linoleum knife is the sharp edge, while it is the *outer edge* of the lead cutter that is sharpened. If you have a knife sharpener at home, you can hone the outer edge of the linoleum knife and it becomes a perfectly adequate tool.

The action of the lead cutter is a gentle rocking motion rather than a slicing or cutting one (Fig. 2–15). As you rock back and forth across the flat (not channeled) surface of the came, you can separate a length without crushing the ends.

Lead Stretcher. If the lead came is not smooth and straight, it should be stretched before you use it. This can be accomplished by means of a special tool called a lead stretcher, but I do not recommend that you buy one, as they cost about $5. The job can be done just as well by two people holding each end of the lead strip with pliers and pulling (Fig. 2–16), or by placing one end in a vise and pulling on the other with pliers. Do not yank or jerk on it—just pull firmly.

You can substitute the flat, unchanneled lead strips that I used for the butterfly within the body of this type of project. You cannot use them as substitutes for the U-shaped lead, however, as the crystals would have nothing to "grab onto" and the outside pieces of lead would fall off the finished project. Soldering is optional when using the flat strips within the framework of a U-channeled lead piece. The strips adhere to the melted plastic, so if the plastic lies on both sides of the strip, the attachment is sturdy.

If your local craft, hobby, or hardware store can't supply the equipment you need, you can obtain catalogues from any of several sources listed in the Sources of Supply section.

Stretching the lead with two pairs of pliers.

BRILLIANT BLUEBIRD

Shown in the color section, Figure 2, this lovely bluebird in flight has simple outlines that make an easy project for your first work with lead cames.

MATERIALS	EQUIPMENT
4 oz. turquoise cooking crystals	soldering iron and holder
small amount of orange or yellow crystals	spool of 60/40 resinous core solder
	cookie sheet
1 opaque black crystal	aluminum foil
10″ length of H came	tweezers and brush
25″ length of U came	metal skewer
	spoon
	pliers
	newspapers
	waxed paper
	blunt pencil or felt tip pen
	soapless steel wool
	sewing thread

1. Lay a length of waxed paper over the pattern in Figure 2–17 and trace the lines with a blunt pencil or felt tip pen. Then lay your waxed paper pattern on a flat working surface with a thick layer of newspapers underneath it for protection.

2. Stretch your lead cames. Since the lead is too unwieldy to get the complete outline shape of the bird in one continuous line, I always divide it into sections that are easy to work with. For the bluebird, the most obvious divisions are each wing and the body; this will give you 3 sections of U-shaped lead to join together later.

In order to determine the length of each piece of lead, lay a strand of thread along each pattern section (Fig. 2–18) and then cut the U came to corresponding lengths. Allow an extra fraction of an inch for *mitering* joints (trimming the ends for a neatly fitting joint before soldering).

3. With the channel of the lead facing inward, use your fingers and the pliers to bend and shape the lead along the outside line defining the shape of the bird. Place the shaped lead cames on top of the waxed paper pattern.

The lead must be clean before the solder will adhere to it, so rub the ends of the strips with steel wool, rinse, and dry thoroughly. Solder the pieces together at the 4 points where the lead strips meet (Fig. 2–17; joints A, B, C, and D). You will also have to solder at the point where the shape of the body joins itself to become one continuous line.

4. Use H came to divide sections of the bird's tail (or any section within the outer shape if you have selected another pattern). Measure and

Fig. 2–17

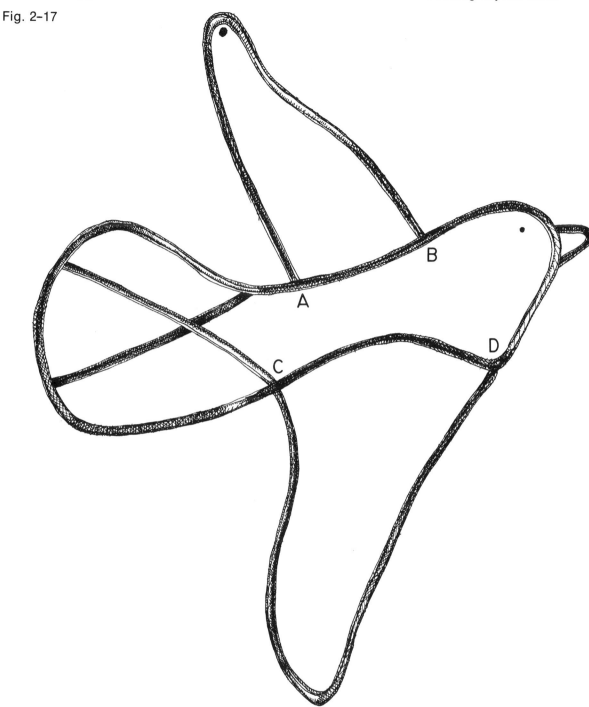

Pattern for the bluebird.

cut the largest pieces first. Therefore, solder first the line running from the upper left of the tail down to the joining of the body with the wing. Use two short lengths of lead to complete the tail.

Fig. 2-18

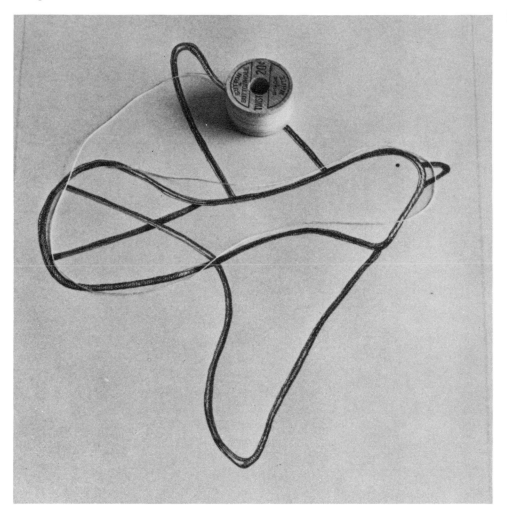

Measuring the outline with thread to determine the length of lead needed.

5. Bend a small piece of U-shaped lead for the beak and solder it onto the frame. Place the lead shape on aluminum foil on a cookie sheet and preheat your oven to 350°.

6. Fill each section of the bird except the beak with turquoise crystals. Nudge the granules directly into the channels of the U and H cames so that the cooking crystals will adhere well to the lead.

Fill the beak with orange or yellow crystals. Use a single opaque black crystal, for the eye, or, if you wish, try a sequin or an Indian bead instead.

7. Bake for approximately 30 minutes—or until done—and allow to cool for 20 to 30 minutes before handling.

8. With a hot skewer or knitting needle, pierce the plastic through the tip of the upper wing. Insert a length of cord or wire through the hole and tie. Suspend the bluebird where he can "fly" freely.

USING LIQUID LEAD

Liquid lead (Craft Steel®) is available in craft and hobby stores. It is generally used as a filler for stained glass, mosaic pieces, or glass and polyester stones. It comes in 6-ounce metal tubes and sells for approximately $1.25 a tube.

The material is *extremely flammable* as it comes from the tube and should not be used near a fire or flame. It takes two or three hours to dry at normal room temperature and after that there is no danger whatsoever in placing it in the oven with cooking crystals.

With liquid lead or Craft Steel, you can make your own designs or trace them from coloring books. The outlines that liquid lead makes are not as attractive as those made of lead strips or cames, but the material is easier to work with. You merely squeeze it right from the tube as you do toothpaste. No cutting or soldering is involved. However, it is not as sturdy as lead and you must use more care with a finished piece to prevent sections from breaking apart.

Because of the waiting period while the designs dry, you may want to trace a number of different liquid lead projects at one time. For example, you could make 10 or 12 small objects from one tube which you could use as Christmas tree ornaments or as package ties. If you have the patience, retrace the first layer and wait another two or three hours. This is not necessary, but a thicker application will produce a sturdier piece.

SYLVESTER THE SEAL

A cute and colorful fellow, Sylvester would make an ideal party favor. Make a dozen or more!

MATERIALS	EQUIPMENT
tube of Craft Steel	waxed paper
small amounts of cooking crystals	tape
in pink, magenta, and green	aluminum foil
cord	cookie sheet
	hot mitts

1. Tape a piece of waxed paper over Sylvester's outline (Fig. 2–19). With an open tube of liquid lead, trace the lines of the pattern directly onto the waxed paper (Fig. 2–20). You can keep better control of the flow if you keep your wrist flat on the paper as you work. Use the liquid lead to draw a loop at the top for hanging.

Let the liquid lead air dry for 2 to 3 hours.

2. When the liquid lead has completely dried, lift or peel it off the waxed paper and lay it on the foil covered cookie sheet.

Fill each section with cooking crystals: pink for Sylvester, green for his eye, magenta and green stripes for the ball.

Pattern for Sylvester the Seal.

3. Place the cookie sheet into a 350° preheated oven and bake for about 15 to 20 minutes.

Remove the cookie sheet from the oven and cool.

4. Tie a length of cord through the loop you made at the top and hang the decoration.

Fig. 2-20

Squeezing liquid lead onto waxed paper (*Craft Steel® manufactured by Magic American Chemical Corp.*).

Using Bamboo Shapes as Frames

Two-dimensional bamboo shapes, in sizes ranging from 6 to 18 inches, are made in Hong Kong and sold in import shops for purely decorative purposes. They generally cost between $1 and $2, depending on size and design. I found that these shapes not only withstand oven heat, but even adhere to the melting Cooking Crystal. So without using any glue or solder, you can adapt these shapes to your own purposes—and greatly enhance them in the process.

If painted with black acrylic spray, the bamboo resembles a lead frame; you can, of course, paint them any color you'd like and the natural bamboo is a lovely complement to the crystals.

When choosing bamboo shapes, try to get the ones that are most nearly flat. Sometimes the wood has a tendency to curl; that would allow the cooking crystals to "escape" from one section to another. If you get a frame that does not rest completely flat, you can soak it for 2 to 3 hours in water and then weigh it down with heavy books until it is dry.

If you have an import shop in your vicinity, you can probably find a wide variety of animal and floral shapes to choose from. If you cannot find the daisy for the next project, or you want a more varied selection, see the Source of Supply listing.

DAISY

The finished bamboo frame daisy is shown in color in Figure 4.

MATERIALS	EQUIPMENT
bamboo daisy	aluminum foil
8 ounces each of cooking crystals in yellow, green, and brown	cookie sheet
	skewer
black acrylic spray paint (optional)	spoon

1. If you want the bamboo frame on the finished piece to resemble the lead stripping of stained glass, spray both sides of the frame with acrylic spray and allow it to dry thoroughly before you proceed. If you're going to leave it in its natural state, go right on with step 2.

2. Lay the frame on a foil-covered cookie sheet and spoon the crystals into each section—yellow petals, brown center, green leaves. Smooth the granules at a depth that is level with the top edge of the bamboo frame as shown in Figure 2–21.

Fig. 2–21

Spooning crystals into a bamboo frame.

3. Bake for 30 minutes—or until done—in a preheated 350° oven; cool for 20 to 30 minutes after removing from the oven.

4. Some of the bamboo shapes have hanging rings on them. If yours does not, pierce the plastic at the top of the daisy with a heated skewer and insert a length of cord for hanging. Hanging with leather thongs gives the bamboo shapes an interesting touch!

MAKING DECORATIONS WITHOUT FRAMES

While the other techniques in this chapter make cooking crystals resemble leaded stained glass, this method makes no such pretensions. It is simple, appealing, and satisfying to children as well as adults—and the end product looks just like plastic!

Fig. 2-22

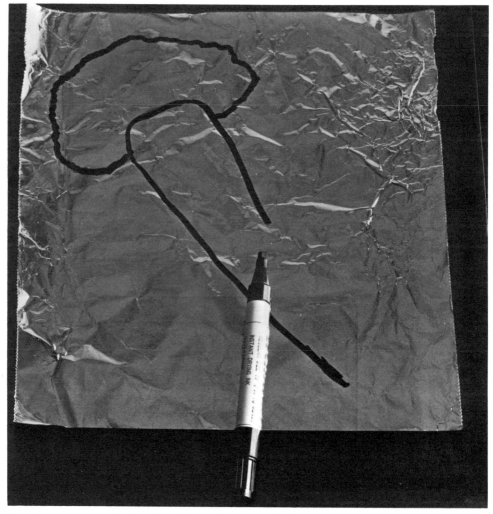

Drawing your own design directly on aluminum foil.

As I stated before, the molten crystals are too viscous to flow freely. Therefore, even without a frame to contain them, the crystals will retain the shape they were placed in with only a minimal amount of spreading. Any colors on top of, or adjacent to, other colors will fuse and become one mass without any dividing seam between them.

The next two projects discuss the methods of making ornaments by drawing freehand designs directly on aluminum foil and transferring coloring book patterns to foil.

DRAWING SHAPES FREEHAND

For this project, plan your design so that it's fairly large and simple, whether whimsical or realistic, and decide upon the colors you want to use.

MATERIALS	EQUIPMENT
cooking crystals in selected colors	aluminum foil
cord	cookie sheet
	hot mitts
	metal skewer
	felt tip pen
	spoon
	brush and tweezers

1. Cover the cookie sheet with a length of aluminum foil large enough to contain the design you want. Remember that the crystals should be placed at least 2 inches from the edge of the foil.

With a felt tip pen or crayon, draw the outline form of any design you wish directly on the foil. Keep any inner section you want to add fairly large and simple without intricate detail, as shown in Fig. 2–22. Be sure that any sections extending from the main body are not so delicate at the attachment point that they might break off.

Do not use a sharp pencil or ballpoint pen which can cause an accordion fold tear in the foil. If the foil should tear, you must throw it away as the melting crystal will surround it and make the foil impossible to remove.

2. With the spoon, begin filling in the spaces to a depth of approximately 1/8 inch. Place adjacent colors next to each other with no space in between (Fig. 2–23). Even up the borders by pushing the granules gently inward with either the brush or the side of your index finger. Brush away any stray granules from the outer edges. As the granules melt, the different colored crystals will adhere to one another and become a solid mass.

3. Bake for 20 to 30 minutes in a preheated 350° oven. When the plastic is smooth, remove the cookie sheet from the oven and let it cool for 20 to 30 minutes before peeling off the aluminum foil.

Fig. 2–23

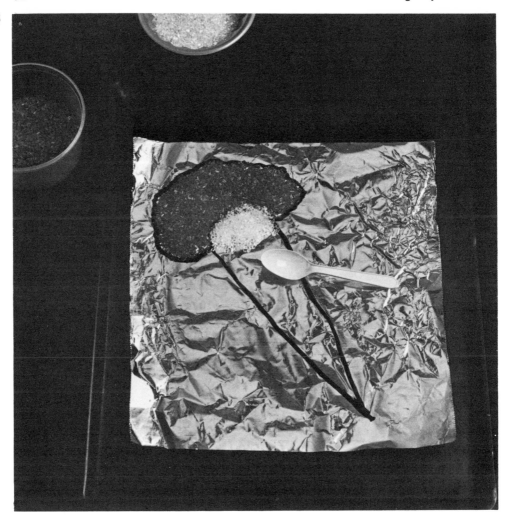

Spooning the crystals into your outline.

4. Wearing a hot mitt, heat the skewer and pierce a hole through the top center of the finished object, a half inch or more from the edge. Thread the cord through the hole and knot it.

TRANSFERRING PATTERNS TO FOIL

The mischievous cat shown in color, Figure 8, is very similar to drawings you might find in a coloring book. The laced shoe shown in Figure 2–24 also makes a delightful ornament. Select any large, clear design you want—a coloring book is an excellent source—or use the cat pattern (Fig. 2–25) or the shoe pattern (Fig. 2–26).

Fig. 2-24

A laced cooking crystal shoe.

MATERIALS	EQUIPMENT
cooking crystals in selected colors	ballpoint pen or sharp pencil
cord	cookie sheet
	aluminum foil
	tweezers
	brush
	hot mitt
	skewer
	spoon
	2 paper clips

1. Place a sheet of aluminum foil larger than the pattern you selected onto your working surface. Place the picture you want to trace on top and fasten it to the foil with paper clips.

2. Trace the lines of the pattern with pen or pencil, using a firm enough pressure to transfer the impression to the foil (Fig. 2–27). Don't bear down so hard that the pen could tear through the paper.

Fig. 2–25

Pattern for the mischievous cat shown in color.

3. Place the foil sheet with the impression of your picture embossed on its surface onto the cookie sheet (Fig. 2–28). If the outlines are hard to follow, retrace the lines with a crayon or felt tip pen.

4. With the spoon, begin filling in the spaces to a height of approximately ⅛ inch. Place each color next to its adjoining one with no space in between. Even up the borders of any one color by pushing the granules gently inward with either the brush or the side of your index finger. Brush away any stray granules from the outer edges. As the granules melt, the different colored crystals will adhere to one another and become one solid mass.

5. Bake for 20 to 30 minutes in a preheated 350° oven (the time depends on the size of your drawing; experience with previous projects will tell you when it's done). When the plastic is smooth, remove the cookie sheet from the oven and let it cool for 20 to 30 minutes before peeling off the foil.

6. Heat the tip of the skewer by holding it in an open flame. Make sure you wear the hot mitt as you do this; the heat travels up the metal skewer. When the tip of the skewer is hot, pierce a hole through the top center of your finished plastic piece. Thread the cord through the hole, knot, and hang the ornament in a window.

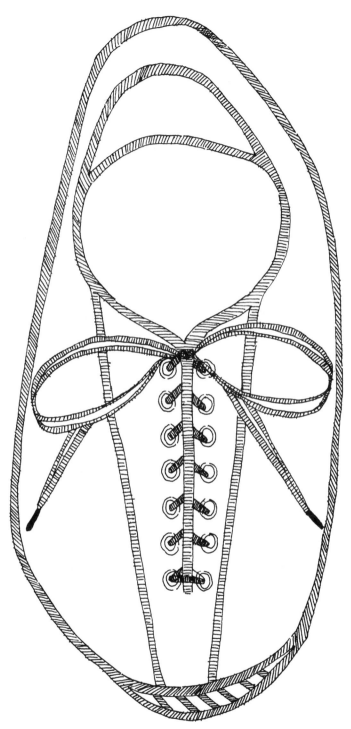

Pattern for making the shoe shown in Fig. 2-24.

Fig. 2-27

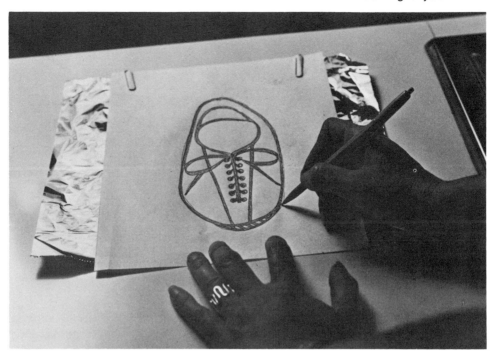

Tracing the pattern onto foil with a firm, gentle pressure.

Fig. 2-28

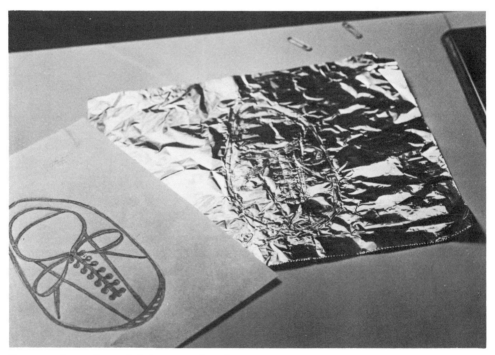

Remove the embossed foil to a cookie sheet.

CHAPTER 3

Using Kitchen Molds

ANY ovenproof container filled with cooking crystals and baked at 350° will produce a solid plastic form in the shape of the container. Most likely to be found in your kitchen are Pyrex® and metal molds: tart, cake, and pie pans; muffin tins; Jell-o® molds; and preformed aluminum foil molds, such as frozen dinner trays. The use of cooking crystals in these containers does not prevent them from being used in food preparation; the crystals are nontoxic. However, we will describe a number of useful containers which you may wish to buy specifically as cooking crystal molds.

Unlike the frames you have been using for the earlier projects, these containers do not attach themselves to the melting plastic. As the plastic cools, you hear cracking and popping noises which signify that the plastic is shrinking away from the sides of the baking dish or container. When completely cooled, the hardened plastic is easily released and the container can be used over and over again. It is never necessary to grease the mold. However, if the mold is not clean before use, the plastic does not drop out as easily. It may then be necessary to gently rap the mold against the kitchen counter or on the floor. Rap gently so as not to dent the mold; the plastic is practically indestructible and will not be damaged.

When choosing kitchen molds, you must eliminate any container which has its brand name stamped on the inside surface. Unfortunately, this makes it necessary to reject molds which otherwise would be perfectly suitable. But the plastic picks up every mark from the container in which it is baked.

Empty tin cans and jar lids often make very useful molds, but you must be careful: if any part of the circumference is smaller than the opening, you won't be able to remove the baked plastic without cutting the container.

For example, the metal lip on the inside rim of most cans makes the opening smaller than the body of the can; some coffee cans have rings of indentations around the center; jar lids generally have threads for screwing them on, etc. Since these are disposable items, however, you may choose to use them and cut them away with metal shears. I just don't want you to make this mistake with something valuable!

Also remember that *you cannot use plastic molds*. They would melt right along with the cooking crystals!

Fig. 3-1

An assortment of metal and Pyrex® pans that make marvelous molds.

The size and shape of the mold will suggest the possible uses to which you can put the finished plastic pieces. Christmas tree decorations, gift ties, window shade pulls, key ring ornaments, pendants, earrings, and charms for bracelets are all obvious trinkets made from the smaller molds. Trays, bowls, medallions, window decorations, and room dividers are only a few of the things that can be made from the larger molds and will be described in greater detail in later chapters. At this point, I will merely describe some of the molds available to you.

Usual and Unusual Molds

Metal and Ovenproof Glass. Cake and pie pans offer a variety of circles, squares, and rectangles which can be used as window decorations, trivets, medallions—whatever your whim. Individual custard cups and deep dish pie containers are two additional circle sizes. Some advantageous shapes are shown in Figure 3–1.

Muffin Tins. A variety of sizes are very convenient molds. You can make six, eight, or twelve circles at one time. Children love to make and

Fig. 3–2

Tart molds with fluted sides.

give them as sets of coasters. These circles are also used to make wind chimes, room dividers, and even lamps.

Tart Molds. Available in an abundant selection of two-inch geometric shapes, tart molds have fluted sides. An assortment of circles, squares, triangles, ovals, and diamonds are shown in Figure 3–2. They are generally available in kitchenware and hardware stores for about 25 cents each. They make delightful Christmas tree decorations and pendants.

Petit fours molds. Available with straight sides (Fig. 3–3) as well as fluted ones (Fig. 3–4), petit fours molds are small—usually about an inch in diameter. They are generally imported from France and are found in kitchen gourmet shops here for approximately 25 cents each. If you are adventurous and patient, you can pay 10 cents each plus postage to order them from a restaurant supply store in Paris (see Source of Supply listing). Some of the styles available are shown here and should be ordered by number as indicated in Figure 3–4. These molds make items small enough to be used as earrings, rings, and pendants. They also make very nice shade pulls and Christmas decorations.

Fig. 3–3

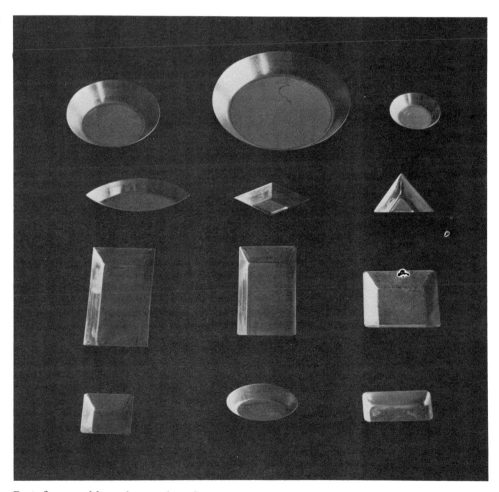

Petit fours molds with straight sides.

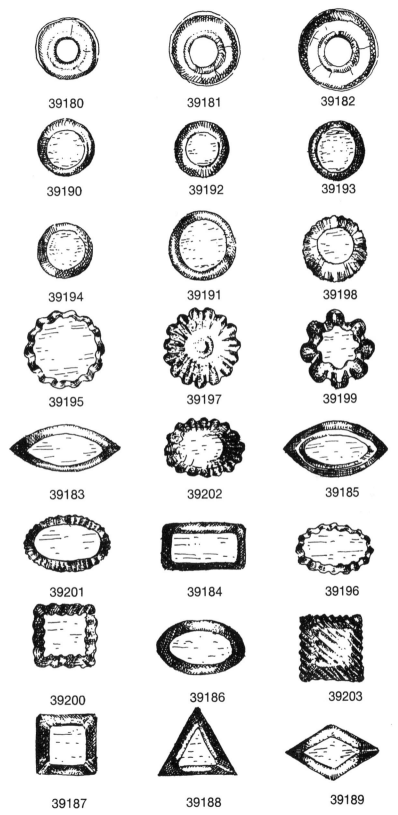

39180   39181   39182

39190   39192   39193

39194   39191   39198

39195   39197   39199

39183   39202   39185

39201   39184   39196

39200   39186   39203

39187   39188   39189

Fancy fluted petit fours molds can be ordered by number from E. Dehillerin (*see Sources of Supply*).

Candy Molds. An assortment of charming animal shapes, as well as geometric designs, are available in small candy molds (Fig. 3–5). Children are especially fond of these for making jewelry and key chains for themselves and for gifts. These molds are difficult to find—a gourmet shop is the best bet, or see Source of Supply listing if you'd like to order by mail.

Toy Baking Pans. Children's "play" cookware includes squares, circles, rectangles, and muffin tins in 3- to 4-inch sizes (Fig. 3–6). These shapes can be useful in almost any project and these convenient sizes are otherwise impossible to find. You should be able to find them in most dime, drug, or toy stores.

Foil Pans. A variety of interesting shapes are available in preshaped aluminum foil pans (Fig. 3–7). In addition to the rounded triangle you find in frozen food packages, you can buy oval, round, square, and rectangular

 Fig. 3–5

Candy molds in assorted designs and animal shapes.

Toy baking pans make wonderful molds for jewelry ornaments.

ones. E-Z-Foil® pans, which are available at supermarket and hardware stores, offer two different cookie sheets as well. Each cookie sheet has nine or ten preshaped animal or Christmas designs that are very appealing; you can also find cake pans in the shape of Santa Claus, a gingerbread man, a fish, and a Christmas tree. All of these foil pans cost about $1 per package.

All of the preceding molds, whether they are filled to the brim with cooking crystals, or just have a layer on the bottom, employ exactly the same method of preparation. I will describe the technique used for molds with flat bottoms first, and then go on to the use of Jell-o molds and cookie cutters, which each have their own unique methods.

Fig. 3-7

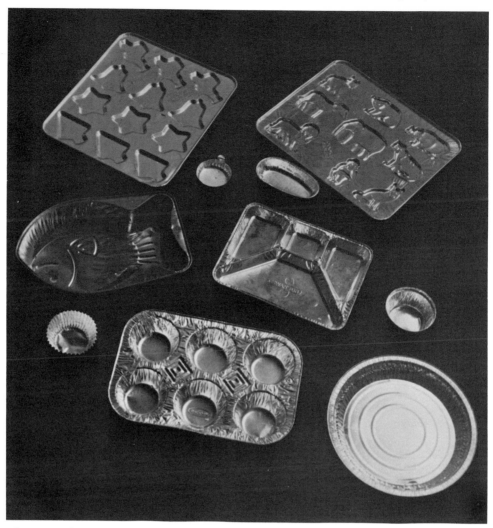

Aluminum foil pans come in a wide selection of patterns.

MAKING ORNAMENTS IN FLAT-BOTTOMED MOLDS

You can use one color or several colors next to each other. More than two colors layered on top of one another tend to look more muddy than attractive. Barely covering the bottom of the mold will produce a fragile, lacy effect. Filling it to the top will produce a sturdy piece.

MATERIALS

several colors of cooking crystals
  in small amounts
cord, leather thong, or chain

EQUIPMENT

molds
cookie sheet
spoon
skewer
hot mitts

1. Spoon the crystals into the molds to the depth you prefer. If the mold is small (in Figure 3–8, you see I used tart pans), I generally recommend filling it to the top. For larger molds, I find that approximately ⅛ to ¼ inch is sufficient.

2. Bake the filled mold at 350° for 10 to 45 minutes, depending on the size of the mold and the depth of the granules. If you are baking a number of small molds at one time, place them on a cookie sheet for your own convenience in placing them in and removing them from the oven.

3. When the plastic looks smooth and glossy, remove the mold from the oven and allow it to cool thoroughly. Remove the plastic from the mold.

4. If you want to hang the finished ornament, heat the skewer over an open flame and pierce the plastic about ¼- to ½-inch from the top. Thread the cord, thong, or chain through the hole.

Fig. 3–8

Several filled tart molds are placed on a larger pan.

MAKING A UNIQUE HORS D'OEUVRE TRAY

I selected the fish design for this project, but any mold you want to choose is fine.

MATERIALS   EQUIPMENT

at least 2 lbs. of cooking crystals   Jell-o mold
                                                           cookie sheet
                                                           skewer
                                                           hot mitts

1. Pour the cooking crystals into the mold so that the entire mold is filled to the top. Because of the many surfaces and facets (or overall design, such as fish, lamb, lobster), you want to capture as much of the mold's likeness as possible (Fig. 3–9).

2. Bake the filled mold at 350° for at least an hour or until the surface looks smooth and glossy. The surface will have become concave because of the shrinkage. Refill the mold with cooking crystals so that the surface is level again and continue baking until all the granules are smooth and blended.

3. Turn the oven temperature off and *let the mold cool inside the oven*. Because of the plastic's bulk, you want it to cool slowly to prevent internal cracking. It should take about 2 to 3 hours before you can remove it from the oven and from the mold.

4. Although this piece could be a purely decorative item, it makes a very attractive and unusual hors d'oeuvre server. Plan the spacing on the top surface for about 24 holes, 1½–2 inches apart. Heat the skewer and puncture each hole to a depth of approximately 1 inch. When company comes, spear each appetizer with a toothpick and place the other end of each toothpick in one of the holes. Quite a conversation piece!

Using Cookie Cutters

Cookie cutters come in so many great sizes and shapes, it's a shame they're not easier to use. The basic problem is that they aren't meant to go into the oven. Some adjustments have to be made in order to use them successfully.

There are basically two types of cutters. The first kind we'll discuss is an outline form which is either soldered or spot welded at the seam. If you can tell that the joint is spot welded, great! You just lay the cookie cutter on a foil-covered pan and fill it with crystals as you would any ordinary mold (Fig. 3–10). If the joint is soldered, however, the solder almost always used commercially is soft and will separate at the 350° required to melt the crystals. Unfortunately, there is almost no way to tell whether a cutter has been soldered or welded except by baking it. If it comes apart, it was soldered! You would have to solder the joint yourself prior to reuse.

Fig. 3-9

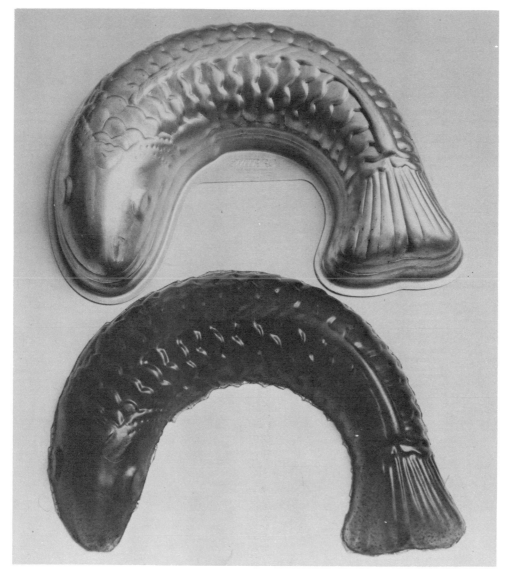

A charming hors d'oeuvre server made from a fish Jell-o® mold.

The second, most common type of cookie cutter has a handle punched out of its top surface. The handle not only prevents the cutter from being turned upside down to act as a container, it creates gaps from which the granules would leak. You must, therefore, use an entirely different approach.

USING COOKIE CUTTERS WITH HANDLES

With so many themes to choose from, you can make ornaments for any holiday or season of the year from cookie cutters.

Fig. 3–10

Baking crystals in outline cookie cutters.

MATERIALS	EQUIPMENT
cooking crystals in several colors	cookie cutters
	cookie sheet
	aluminum foil
	hot mitts

1. Place a piece of aluminum foil (about 6 x 6 inches for one cutter) shiny side up on a flat pan or cookie sheet.

Pour a layer of crystals about ⅛-inch thick, and just larger than the area circumscribed by the cookie cutter, onto the center of the foil. Do not attempt to press out the shape in the unbaked crystal and do not put the cutter in the oven.

Fig. 1
Multicolored butterfly is made from
preformed lead shapes and **strips**
filled with cooking crystals.

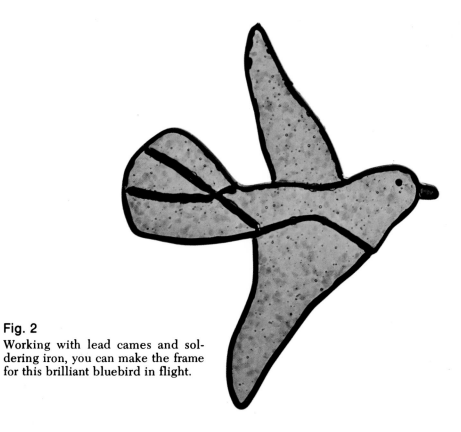

Fig. 2
Working with lead cames and soldering iron, you can make the frame
for this brilliant bluebird in flight.

Fig. 3
Red plastic beads are embedded in crystals before baking to produce a handsome Christmas wreath.

Fig. 4
A preformed bamboo shape is filled with crystals to make this unique daisy.

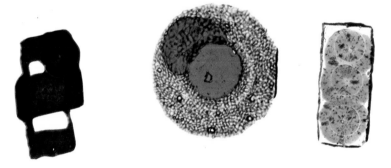

Fig. 5
Fused mosaics produce beautiful designs you can use for medallions and pendants or hang as sun catchers.

2. Place the pan with only the crystals and foil on it into a 350° oven and bake for approximately 15 to 20 minutes, until the plastic looks like a glassy puddle.

3. Put the hot mitts on your hands, open the oven door, and firmly press out the cookie shape while the soft plastic is still in the oven! Leave the cutter in the melted plastic (Fig. 3–11).

Immediately remove the cookie sheet from the oven and allow it to cool for about 15 minutes. After this period of time, lift off the cutter. The excess plastic will be brittle enough to easily break away from the object (Fig. 3–12). You don't need to apply much pressure; the pieces just snap off.

Fig. 3–11

Pressing out shapes while the plastic is hot.

Fig. 3–12

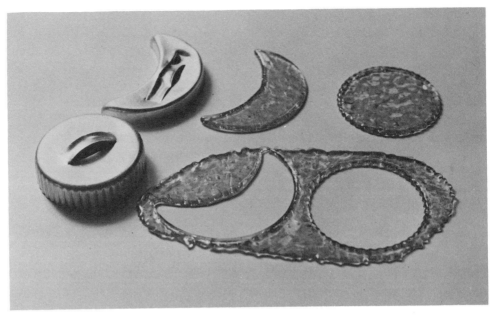

The excess plastic breaks away easily when cooled.

MAKING COOKIE CUTTER SHAPES WITH LEAD CAMES

Any kind of cookie cutter can be used as a pattern around which you bend U-channel lead cames. This is a very satisfactory method since it is easy, does not affect the cookie cutter, and provides a very professional looking finished piece (Fig. 3–13).

MATERIALS	EQUIPMENT
cooking crystals in assorted colors	cookie sheet
U-channel lead (allow 10″ for each shape)	aluminum foil
	soldering iron
cord	60/40 resinous core solder
	thread or string
	lead cutter
	pliers
	hot mitts
	skewer
	cookie cutters

1. Measure the outer perimeter of the cookie cutter with a length of thread or string. Lay the thread along the lead came and cut the lead to size, then stretch the lead strip.

2. Bend the lead around the cookie cutter with the channel facing inward to conform to its shape.

Fig. 3-13

Cookie cutter shapes in frames made from lead cames.

Fig. 3-14

Shape the lead around the cutter, solder the lead and remove the cutter, then fill the shape with crystals.

Lay the cookie cutter and the lead shape on a foil-covered cookie sheet. Solder the ends of the lead strip and remove the cookie cutter (Fig. 3–14). Make sure the lead shape lies flat on the cookie sheet.

If you wish, you can make sections within the lead frame by cutting and soldering H-channel lead cames or lead strips to fit.

3. Fill the shape with cooking crystals and bake in a 350° oven for about 20 minutes or until done. Remove the cookie sheet from the oven and allow to cool for about 15 minutes.

4. Heat the skewer and pierce a hole through the top of the ornament. Attach the cord and hang.

CHAPTER 4

Embedding Objects in Crystals

PRACTICALLY anything can be permanently embedded in cooking crystals. The list includes all the traditional craft items and the method is nearly the same for all of them. A layer of crystal is poured on the bottom of a pan or mold; the item or items to be embedded are laid on the crystal, and another layer of crystal is poured on top. Think of it as a sandwich, with the two layers of crystal serving as the bread and the embedment as the filling. I often use transparent (clear, colorless) or light colored crystals so that the embedment can be seen more clearly as the focal point of the piece.

The various types of embedments are broken down into groups in order to discuss specific problems relating to each group. Naturally, once you are familiar with the properties of each type, you can combine two or more of these categories in any one project. Also, consider the use of embedments as a technique rather than as an end in itself. You can embed materials in any of the shapes or molds I described in earlier chapters, or in any of the projects described throughout this book, as well as working them into your own creations. I will discuss each type of embedment, then present a project using that type. You may want to read through the chapter first, and with this information in mind, combine groups of embedment in a single piece or perhaps use a group III embedment in the trivet.

EMBEDDING SOLID OBJECTS

Group I. The first type of embedment poses no problem. The list includes glass gems, jewels, beads, roundels, marbles, coins, colored stones or gravel, pieces of stained glass, yarn, glitter, buttons, hardware, seashells, ribbon—anything that will not burn or melt in the oven heat when embedded in the crystals.

TRIVET

I used glass jewels in the trivet. Any group I selection is fine.

MATERIALS	EQUIPMENT
1 lb of clear crystals	8″ clean or new pie pan
any embedding materials	hot mitts
from group I	spoon
	cookie sheet (optional)

1. Pour a ⅛-inch layer of crystal into the pie pan, completely covering the bottom of the pan.

2. Place the items to be embedded on top of the layer of crystal in an arrangement that pleases you, as shown in Figure 4–1.

3. Gently spoon on another layer of crystal so as not to disturb your arrangement (Fig. 4–2). Make the crystal as level as possible and be sure to completely cover all the embedments.

 Fig. 4–1

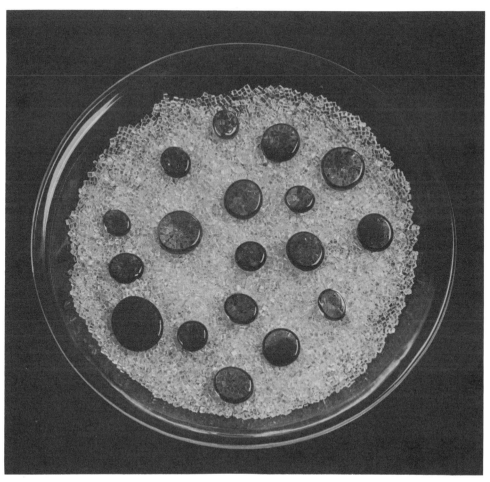

Items to be embedded are placed on a layer of crystals.

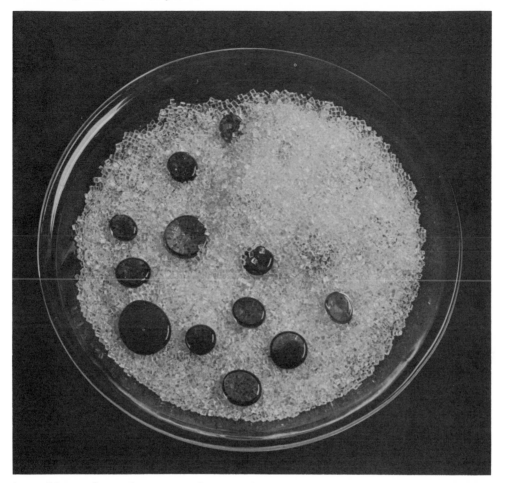

Second layer of crystals is spooned over embedments.

4. Place the pan on a cookie sheet if you like; bake at 350° for approximately 45 minutes or until the plastic looks glossy.

Remove the pan from the oven and allow it to cool for 20 to 30 minutes before removing the plastic from the pan.

5. If the plastic has crept up the sides of the pan so that the piece is not flat on top and bottom, place the piece on a flat cookie sheet with the uneven edges down. Return it to a 350° oven for approximately 5 minutes. The edges will have melted down and the piece will be uniform on both sides.

Embedding Plastic Items or Pieces

Group II. This group includes anything made of plastic: beads, jewels, sequins, buttons, flowers, toy objects, even pieces of previously baked crystal (such as the broken off pieces left from cookie cutter designs or the mosaic pieces you will learn about in a later chapter). Plastic pieces can be embedded successfully, but expect them to melt into dots or blobs of color rather than retain their original shapes. You can effectively use them to get polka dots, spots of color, and eyes.

CHRISTMAS WREATH

The wreath is shown in the color section, Figure 3, and makes a lovely holiday addition to your home.

MATERIALS	EQUIPMENT
½ lb. light green cooking crystals	8″ bundt pan
25 opaque red plastic cartwheel beads	hot mitts
	skewer
a stick-on red ribbon bow	
cord	

1. Scatter 10 of the beads on the bottom of the bundt pan. Pour half the crystal over the beads so that the bottom of the pan is covered.

Scatter 10 more beads over the crystal (Fig. 4–3). Pour the remaining crystal over them, then place the remaining 5 beads on top.

2. Place the bundt pan into a 350° oven and bake for approximately 45 minutes.

Remove the pan from the oven when the crystal is glossy and allow it to cool for approximately 20 to 30 minutes before turning the wreath from the pan. The uneven edges around the wreath resemble irregular branches and make it look more "real."

3. Heat the skewer in an open flame, being sure to wear the hot mitts. Puncture 2 holes in the plastic ½-inch down from the top edge with a ½-inch space between them.

Thread the cord through the 2 holes and tie it into a tight knot for hanging. Remove the backing from the bow and place it on the wreath to cover the holes. You might wish to hang the wreath in the window, from the mantle, or on the door.

Embedding Nature Finds

Group III. Leaves, ferns, flowers, or parts of plants can be embedded, but they must be dried before use. Plants with moisture still in them have a tendency to turn brown in the baking process. Also, escaping moisture causes bubbles to be captured within the confines of the plastic; this results in large, unattractive craters in the finished product.

You can buy packages of dried leaves, ferns, and even butterfly wings at your hobby store. These can be used directly from the package with no prior preparation.

You can also prepare your own fresh leaves, ferns, and flowers by drying them out in silica gel. This is a chemical which removes the

Fig. 4-3

Plastic beads embedded in crystal.

moisture from plants while allowing them to keep their natural color and shape. It is packaged by a number of companies and is available at most craft and hobby stores.

NATURE CRAFT PLACE MAT

The place mat is shown in color in Figure 6. I prefer to use transparent cooking crystals so that the nature finds are displayed more prominently.

MATERIALS	EQUIPMENT
1½ to 2 lbs. of cooking crystals	jelly roll pan
dried ferns or leaves	hot mitts
butterfly wings	spoon

1. Be sure to use a jelly roll pan, not a cookie sheet. A jelly roll pan has a rim about ½-inch high on all sides. Make sure the pan is either new or clean because you will be using it without aluminum foil.

Pour a single layer of crystal over the entire surface of the pan, no more than ⅛ inch deep.

2. Arrange the ferns and wings attractively on top of the crystals as shown in Figure 4-4.

Fig. 4-4

Arranging ferns and butterfly wings on crystals.

Gently spoon another thin layer of crystal over the ferns and wings so that they are completely covered. Smooth the crystals so that they are as level as possible.

3. Bake in a 350° oven for approximately 30 to 45 minutes. Remove the pan from the oven when the plastic looks smooth and glossy. Allow it to cool for 15 to 20 minutes before turning the plastic sheet out of the pan.

If the upper surface is not perfectly flat or if the edges show signs of creeping, replace the plastic sheet upside down in the jelly roll pan. Return it to the oven for about 10 minutes. Allow it to cool again and remove it from the pan.

Repeat the process until you have the number of place mats you want.

EMBEDDING PAPER PRODUCTS

Group IV. Surprisingly enough, just about any kind of paper bakes in cooking crystals without burning or turning brown. This means you can permanently embed mementoes, collections, or souvenirs. The list of paper products that can be embedded includes postage stamps, matchbook covers, cocktail napkins, photographs, and newspaper and magazine clippings. You can also permanently embed invitations, greeting cards, and announcements. You can incorporate art and decoupage prints, foil designs and lettering, colored art papers, and doilies within your designs. Just be certain that you want the items permanently embedded; you cannot remove or reclaim them after the plastic has been baked.

If you use postage stamps or anything that has glue on the back, you must remove the glue from the articles before embedding them (the glue will burn and turn brown). Soak the embedments in water overnight, then place them between blotters and weigh them down with books to dry without curling for the same period of time.

Fig. 4–5

Stamps are inserted upside down (*left*) to make the paperweight.

STAMP COLLECTOR'S PAPERWEIGHT

The finished paperweight is shown in Figure 4–5, along with the embedment process.

MATERIALS	EQUIPMENT
10–12 stamps	A Pyrex custard cup
½ lb. clear or light-colored cook-	hot mitts
ing crystals	spoon

1. Prepare the stamps as described above, removing the glue before you begin.

Pour cooking crystals into the custard cup to a height of approximately 1 inch. Keep in mind that the bottom of the mold will be the top of the paperweight. Therefore, as you fill the mold, the backs of the stamps are toward you and the faces of the stamps are down (Fig. 4–5).

Mound a spoonful of crystal against the side of the mold. Insert a stamp at least ⅛-inch in from the edge and spoon more crystal around it to hold it in place.

Continue placing the remaining stamps into the mold. Try to place them at different angles and at different distances from the center. Fill the mold completely, covering all stamps with at least ¼-inch of crystals.

2. Bake the mold at 350° for about 25 minutes. Refill the cavity with more crystal to level off the botttom, if necessary, and continue baking for another 15 to 20 minutes.

When the plastic is smooth and glossy, remove the mold from the oven and allow it to cool for about 20 minutes before removing the paperweight from the mold.

3. If any crystal granules crept up the sides of the mold and the bottom of the paperweight does not sit perfectly flat, return it to the oven bottom down on a foil-covered pan for approximately 5 to 10 minutes or until the uneven edges have smoothed down.

TISSUE PAPER "HAPPY FACE"

Colored tissue paper, because it is translucent, is more compatible with the transparency of cooking crystals than other papers. The colors blend when overlapped and interesting shaded or mosaic pictures can be made by embedding torn or cut pieces of tissue in the unbaked crystal.

Try something as simple as three concentric circles of different sizes in interesting color combinations such as purple, red, and orange, or three shades of green, or pink, orange, and yellow. Just lay the three circles out, partially overlapping one another, within two layers of crystal.

Even more exciting—especially for young children—is drawing and coloring pictures with felt tip markers on either white or pastel tissue paper. Grandmothers adore receiving trays or trivets made in this fashion, and the "happy face" I made for the next project (see color section, Figure 13) can be used as a trivet.

If you prefer a different design, you can work with a square cake pan or rectangular jelly roll pan; the instructions will serve just as well for any design you might want to draw on tissue paper.

MATERIALS	EQUIPMENT
clear or pastel cooking crystals	12″ pizza pan
white or pastel tissue paper	felt tip markers
	scissors
	hot mitts
	spoon

1. Cut a piece of tissue paper so that it is ¼-inch smaller than the pizza pan on all sides.

With felt tip markers, draw and color any picture or design on the tissue paper (Fig. 4–6).

2. Spoon a layer of crystals into the pan to a depth of ⅛-inch. Lay the tissue paper drawing *upside down* on the crystals (Fig. 4–7).

Spoon a second layer of crystals on top of the tissue paper so that it is completely covered.

3. Bake in a 350° oven for approximately 30 minutes. Remove the pan from the oven when the plastic is transparent and glossy and allow it to cool for about 15 minutes.

If desired, you can pierce two holes in the top for hanging in a window, but this piece makes a very efficient and gay trivet or tray.

MORE SUGGESTIONS FOR EMBEDDING PAPER

Construction Paper Cutouts. You might want to plan an abstract design or a realistic picture—perhaps a whole scene—cutting the components from colored construction paper. An interesting project for a youngster might be an entire barnyard scene, replete with various animals and a big red barn; or perhaps a classroom scene, trying to capture in silhouette the features of various classmates (you can draw in details with magic markers or crayons, but they will not show up especially well in the baked crystals). The procedure for embedding and baking the project is the same as for the tissue face: the only rules are to keep the paper at least ¼-inch from the edges of the pan and be sure the paper is completely covered underneath and on top with crystals—the rest is up to your imagination!

Lettering. By using lettering aids, which are available at stationery and artist supply stores, you can make personalized medallions which are combination greeting cards and gifts (Fig. 4–8). They also make terrific party favors, doing double service as place markers. You can spell out simple messages or individual names and combine the letters with any pictures of your liking.

The letters are available in a large variety of type styles, sizes, and even colors. There are a number of different brands and some of them have asterisks, arrows, diamonds, border designs, etc. as well as letters. You may find these fun to use.

Fig. 4–6

Drawing on tissue paper with felt tip markers.

Fig. 4–7

Place the drawing upside down on the layer of crystals.

Artist-Aid® and Plas-Stick® are fairly typical of the vinyl self-sticking variety (Fig. 4–8). Each letter peels off a backing sheet and is placed upside down and from right to left across the bottom layer of cooking crystal. The adhesive is little affected by the baking process; however, the

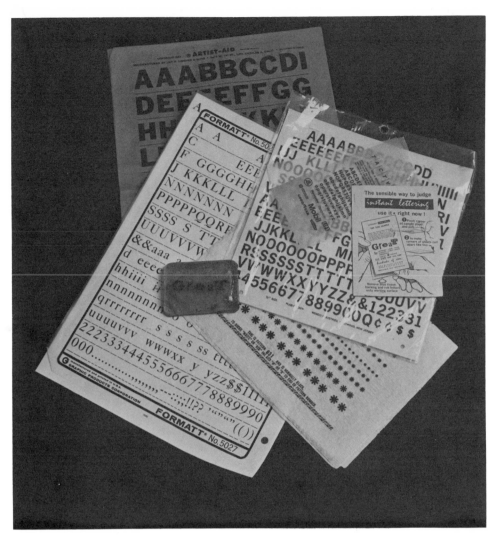

Lettering aids can be used as embedments in crystals.

heat does tend to distort the vinyl plastic. The distortion is never enough to ruin the readability of the letters, but they do change in size from the original.

Letraset® uses a different process to transfer letters. The letters are backed by paper rather than plastic, and no adhesive is involved. Therefore, there will be no distortion. In all instances, be sure the crystals completely cover the embedment.

Covering Back Sides. If you are making a two-dimensional plaque or medallion using letters or newspaper and magazine clippings, it may be desirable for only the front side to be visible. You should blank out the reverse side *before* baking by painting the reverse side of the clipping with black paint, or by laying a piece of black art paper between the back side of the clipping and the top layer of crystal. Remember that the front of the finished plaque or medallion is the bottom of the mold if you use any of the small tart, petit fours, or candy molds.

Another method is to use either white or black opaque crystals for the top layer—or as part of the top layer. Just spread a layer of transparent crystals on the bottom of the mold or pan, lay the cutouts or lettering face downward on top of the transparent crystals, and cover only the necessary parts (or the entire suface) with opaque crystals to hide the reverse side of the picture or the back side of the letters. You can use transparent crystal for the remainder.

If you have already completed a plaque or medallion which has an unattractive back side and you now wish to cover it, aluminum foil is perfect. Its bright surface shines through the transparent areas of crystal while still covering up the objectionable reverse side. Cut the foil to the proper shape and size, with an extra quarter inch on all sides. Make a diagonal cut at all four corners and fold under the quarter-inch margins so that excess foil is not visible from the front side (Fig. 4–9). Spread any household glue along the entire length of the margins and glue them to the back of the plaque or medallion.

Partially Embedding Objects That Can't Be Baked

You may sometimes wish to partially embed objects for three-dimensional or special effects. This may be done in several different ways.

If the item to be partially embedded will not take the oven's heat without burning or melting (such as plastic or organic materials), wait until the crystals have fused into a glossy mass. While the crystals are still in the oven or immediately upon removal, push the object to be embedded into the soft plastic. As the plastic cools and hardens, that part of the object within the plastic becomes permanently attached. It is also possible to just glue things onto the surface of a cooled, hardened piece by using jewelry cement or transparent glue.

FEATHERED CHICKEN

The partial embedments for this project are feathers and a plastic eye.

MATERIALS	EQUIPMENT
½ lb. yellow crystals	cookie sheet
small amount of orange crystals	aluminum foil
5 yellow hackle feathers	crayon
a plastic movable eye	hot mitts
	tweezers or skewer
	spoon

1. Lay a piece of foil shiny side up on the cookie sheet. Use a crayon or felt tip marker to draw the outline shape of the chicken on the foil.

Fig. 4-9

Foil used to cover the back side of a finished project.

Fig. 4-10

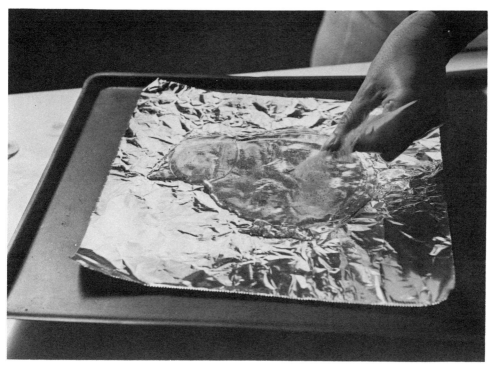

Inserting feathers into the hot plastic.

2. Spoon the yellow crystals to a depth of ⅛-inch within the outlines of the chicken's body and the orange crystals within the outlines of the beak and feet.

3. Place the cookie sheet into a 350° oven for approximately 30 minutes.

When the crystal is smooth and glossy, open the oven door and jab the shafts of the 5 feathers into the body of the chicken at a 30° angle so that the fluffy parts of the feathers look as though they are "growing" toward the back (Fig. 4–10).

4. Remove the cookie sheet from the oven. Wait 2 seconds and then press the plastic eyes into place while the plastic is still soft (Fig. 4–11). Use the tweezers or the skewer as a tool if necessary.

Note: Plastic moving eyes are available in various sizes at the notions counter of any dime store as well as at craft and hobby stores. A bag of 12 to 20 of them costs about 25¢.

Bags of hackle feathers in assorted colors cost about 75¢ for ½ ounce (That's a lot of feathers!) and can be bought at a craft or a hobby store. If you cannot find them, see Source of Supply listing.

Fig. 4-11

Pressing the plastic eye into the warm plastic.

PARTIALLY EMBEDDING OBJECTS THAT CAN BE BAKED

If the objects to be partially embedded can be baked without any harm to them (such as shells, metal, or glass pieces), they may be arranged in the unbaked crystals and placed in the oven with no problem. When the piece is removed from the oven, the areas that were covered with crystals will be embedded and the exposed areas will be visible above the surface of the plastic.

LITTERED LANDSCAPE

MATERIALS	EQUIPMENT
an empty soft drink or beer can	cookie sheet
½ lb. each turquoise, yellow, and	aluminum foil
olive green cooking crystals	metal cutters
54″ length of U-channel lead	lead cutter
110″ length of H-channel lead	soldering iron, and holder
	60/40 resinous core solder
	spoon
	hot mitts
	pliers

1. Open the soft drink or beer can so that the half showing the label and the top and bottom of that half are all intact. Cut the empty can completely in half lengthwise, using the metal cutters (Fig. 4–12).

2. Stretch the U came and shape it into a 12 x 15 inch rectangle with rounded, rather than right angle, corners. Cut off any extra lead and solder the ends of the frame together.

3. Cover the cookie sheet with a single length of aluminum foil and lay the frame on the foil. As shown in Figure 4–13, place the half can in the frame so that it will cover the last grid to the right (3 inches in from the right and 2 inches up from the bottom).

4. Cut the grids of H-channel lead as follows: one 15 inches long, two 10 inches long, two 2½ inches long, three 12 inches long, and one 4½ inches long.

Place the grids within the frame as shown in Figure 4–13 so that you have 3-inch squares. Solder all joinings of the grids where they abut and where they meet the frame. It is not necessary to solder the joining of the beer can.

5. Cut a 4-inch length of H came and fashion it into a circle. Solder the ends of the circle and place it in the top row of grids, second from the left.

Cut and shape sections of H-channel lead to form the outline of the mountain top. Solder each section into place.

6. Spoon the crystals into each section, making sure that the channels in the lead cames are well filled. Make the hill and ground green, the sky

Fig. 4-12

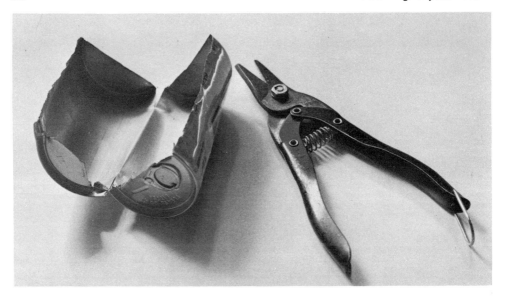

An empty can is cut in half lengthwise.

turquoise, and the moon yellow, filling each area to a depth of ¼-inch. The beer can will be held in place (or embedded) by the melted plastic.

7. Bake in a 350° oven for approximately 45 minutes or until the plastic is smooth and glossy. Remove from the oven and cool.

If desired, you can bend half-inch lengths of heavy wire into loops for hanging. Solder them to the back of the picture at the top of each end grid.

PARTIALLY EMBEDDING WIRE DETAIL AND DECORATION

Wire can be legs, arms, whiskers, antennae, stems, curls—it can, in fact, be any appendage or appurtenance that you can bend or twist into shape.

If the cooking crystal shape is drawn on foil, if the wire shapes are not complicated, and if the wire shapes extend toward the sides rather than up so that they can rest on the pan and not depend on the tacky granules for support you can insert the ends of the wire into the crystal before baking: just a half inch or so of the wire is embedded, while the major portion of the wire is not. If these ends are firmly embedded, you can later move or adjust the position of the wires without fear of their becoming detached.

If the cooking crystals are baked in a mold or small pan where the wires cannot extend toward the sides, you do not embed the wires until after the baking process. Later, when the finished piece is removed from its mold, the wire ends are heated in the same way that the skewer is for the purpose of puncturing holes. However, this time you do not remove the heated wires; you just leave them in place and the surrounding plastic will hold them.

Fig. 4–13

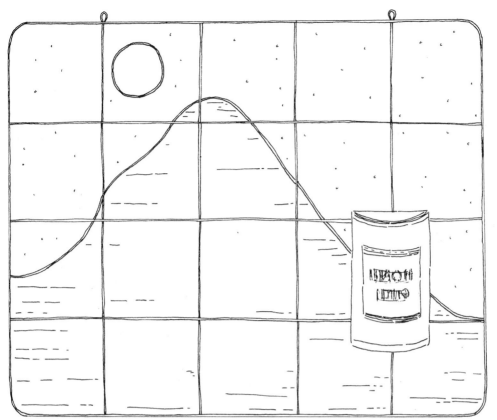

Layout for littered landscape.

LADYBUG

The finished ladybug—ready to fly away home—is shown in Figure 4–14.

MATERIALS	EQUIPMENT
12–20 ¼″ black plastic beads	cookie sheet
½ lb. of red cooking crystals	aluminum foil
4 feet of black 14 gauge wire	felt tip pen
	spoon
	pliers
	wire cutters
	hot mitts

1. Lay the foil on the cookie sheet. Draw the outline shape of the ladybug on the center of the foil with the felt tip pen, making the body a 6-inch oval and the head a 3-inch circle.

2. Arrange all the beads but 2 on the body to represent the ladybug's spots (Fig. 4–15). Two are reserved for the eyes, which you will insert later.

Fig. 4–14

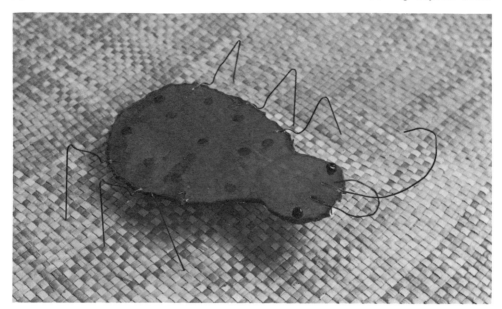

Finished ladybug with partially embedded wire.

Fig. 4–15

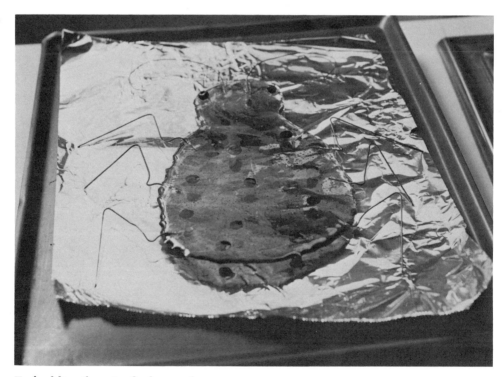

Embedding the wire for legs and antennae.

Spoon ⅛-inch layer of crystals into the head and body areas. Do not bury the beads, but make sure they are surrounded by crystals on all sides.

3. Cut the wire into 8 pieces, each 6 inches long: 6 for the legs and 2 for the antennae. Use the pliers to bend the wire into shape. The legs

should be bent 3 inches from one end and about an inch from the other; the antennae should be curled at the ends (see Fig. 4–15).

4. Place 3 legs on each side of the body and place the 2 antennae at the top of the head. About a half inch of the end of each wire should lie on top of the crystals. Cover these ends with more crystals so that they are completely embedded.

5. Bake at 350° for approximately 30 minutes.

Remove the cookie sheet from the oven and immediately place an eye on either side of the head. Press them into the molten plastic so that they protrude somewhat. Allow the piece to cool for about 20 minutes before peeling away the foil. Then adjust the wires if necessary.

A PRETTY LADY

In this project, I combined an embedded tissue paper drawing and partially embedded wire curls.

MATERIALS	EQUIPMENT
½ lb. clear crystals	8″ pie pan or 12″ pizza pan
7½″ or 11½″ circle of tissue paper	felt tip markers
7 ft. gold color jewelry wire	scissors
	pencil
	ruler
	garden gloves
	hot mitts

1. Draw and color the face and hair of a lady on the circle of tissue paper with felt tip markers. Be sure to color the hair yellow to match the gold curls of wire. (If you use heavier black wire, then of course you would color the hair black.)

2. Pour a layer of crystals to cover the bottom of the pizza or pie pan. Lay the drawing face down on top of the crystals and pour another layer on top of the drawing.

3. Bake in a 350° oven for approximately 30 minutes.

Meanwhile, cut the wire into 7 even 1-foot lengths. Twist each length around a pencil. When you slip the coil of wire off the pencil, it still retains its spiral bounce. These are your 7 curls (Fig. 4–16).

When the plastic looks smooth and shiny, remove the pan from the oven and allow it to cool for about 20 minutes before turning the plastic piece out.

4. Wearing the garden gloves, heat the ends of the wire curls, one at a time, in a gas flame. As the wire gets red hot, jab it into the plastic and leave it there. As the plastic surrounding the wire cools, it permanently holds or embeds the wire. Three curls are placed at the forehead and two are placed on either side of the head.

Fig. 4-16

Wire curls are heated and pressed into plastic surface.

CHAPTER 5

Fusing and Mosaics

YOU have already discovered that plastic cooking crystals can be baked and rebaked several times without doing any damage to them. Each time the solid plastic is returned to the oven, it softens and fuses to the plastic pieces or granules adjacent to it. The whole then solidifies into one mass when it is removed from the oven and cooled.

You can use this property to your advantage by prebaking crystals in molds or by cutting or scoring (see Ch. 6) the molten crystals to make your own mosaic shapes. These shapes are then assembled into a picture, design, or decoration which is returned to the oven for final fusing.

Shapes can be made as whim dictates, later working the pieces into an abstract or geometric design however they fit pleasingly together. Or you can predetermine your design or picture and make shapes to fit it. I will discuss both methods in the following projects.

Knowing about this fusing technique eliminates wasted plastic. You don't have to discard broken pieces, mistakes, or bad designs. Just reheat the plastic, score it into smaller pieces, and incorporate them into mosaic pictures.

MAKING MOSAICS IN MOLDS FOR ORNAMENTS

MAKING THE PLASTIC SHAPES

When selecting your colors, have the finished ornaments in mind. You may want Christmas colors, or shades that blend with room furnishings for permanent decorations.

MATERIAL	EQUIPMENT
cooking crystals in a variety of colors	12-cup toy muffin tin hot mitts spoon

1. Spoon a thin layer of cooking crystal into the bottom of each of the muffin tin cups.

2. Place the muffin tin into the oven at 350° until the crystals fuse. It is not necessary to bake the crystal to its final glossy stage, since you can do that in the second baking.

3. Allow the discs to cool about 15 minutes and turn them out of the muffin tin.

MAKING MOSAIC DECORATIONS FROM YOUR SHAPES

Several attractive arrangements are shown in Figure 5–1, but the possibilities are unlimited.

MATERIALS	EQUIPMENT
12 plastic discs nylon cord	cookie sheet aluminum foil hot mitts skewer

1. Lay a single length of aluminum foil on the cookie sheet. Arrange the plastic discs on the foil in one of the following arrangements shown in Figure 5–1 or in an arrangement of your own creation.

Left: 6 discs overlapping one another to form a circle
      1 disc radiating outward from each of the inner circles
Center: 4 discs overlapping to form a circle
      4 additional discs placed over the seams
      4 discs placed on top of the last group's seams

Fig. 5-1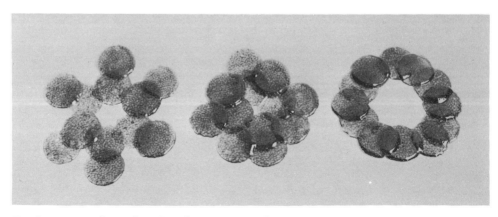

Twelve mosaic discs placed in three suggested arrangements.

Right: 6 discs, not touching, but placed in a circle
          6 remaining discs centered on the spaces between the
          original circles

2. Place the cookie sheet into a 350° oven and bake for about 10 to 15 minutes—or until the discs are fused into one solid piece.

Remove the cookie sheet from the oven and cool for about twenty minutes.

3. Heat the end of the metal skewer. Pierce a hole through the top of the decoration and thread a length of cord through the hole. Hang the decoration from the Christmas tree or in a window.

MAKING A FLOWER WITH MOSAIC PIECES

MAKING THE MOSAICS

If you want to make the flower in the second part of this project with your mosaic pieces, use this first stage to make the green diamonds and circles, as well as the red and green "free" shapes in the quantities noted in the materials listing for the flower.

Fig. 5–2

Scoring the hot plastic with a food chopper.

MATERIAL   EQUIPMENT

½ lb. cooking crystals in green   cookie sheet
    and red   aluminum foil
                                     hot mitts
                                     food chopper, pizza cutter, or knife
                                     assorted glasses, jars, empty cans,
                                         hollow piping
                                     spoon
                                     mosaic tile snippers (optional)

    1. Cover the cookie sheet with one length of aluminum foil.

    The cookie sheet is large enough to bake 2 colors of plastic at the same time, so cover a 6 x 10 inch area with red crystals, and use the other end for green crystals, spooning them to a depth of ⅛- to ¼-inch.

    2. Place the cookie sheet into a 350° oven for about 30 minutes—or until the plastic appears smooth and shiny.

    You have more time to work if you leave the pan in the oven, so open the oven door, and with hot mitts on your hands, use the chopper, pizza cutter, or knife to cut parallel lines deeply in the hot plastic. Work very quickly. Cut across lines at right angles to make squares or rectangles; cut diagonally to make diamonds or triangles (Fig. 5–2). The strands of plastic that lift up with your knife or chopper will break off when they are cooled.

Fig. 5–3

Making circles in hot plastic with glasses.

Use round glasses, jars, empty cans, pipe of various diameters, or cookie cutters to cut different size circles in the hot plastic. Leave these tools in the molten plastic until the plastic hardens (**Fig. 5–3**).

Fig. 5–4

Break the plastic along the score lines.

Fig. 5–5

Pressing out the circles.

3. Remove the cookie sheet from the oven and allow the plastic to cool for about 20 minutes. Then lift one color area off the foil and break the plastic along the score lines (Fig. 5–4). They are similar to crackers that are perforated and should break apart quite easily. If a piece resists, lay the score along a table edge and then snap downwards. If the circles do not punch out easily, break off the surrounding pieces in tangents (Fig. 5–5). Pieces can also be cut with mosaic tile snippers.

Repeat this process until you have enough mosaic pieces in as many colors as you need.

USING MOSAICS TO MAKE A FLOWER

A suggested arrangement of mosaic pieces for a "mod" flower is shown in Figure 5–6; you may vary the shapes and arrangement in any way.

MATERIALS	EQUIPMENT
16 green ¾" diamond shaped mosaics	cookie sheet
	aluminum foil
15 red 1" x 2" mosaics (rectangles or "free" shapes)	compass
	paper
1 green ½" x 6" oblong mosaic	scissors
2 green 1½" circles	ruler
½ lb. clear cooking crystals	felt tip pen
small amount of yellow cooking crystals	spoon
	hot mitts
	wooden spoon

1. Cover the cookie sheet with a length of aluminum foil. With the felt tip pen, draw a rectangle on the foil that measures 10 x 15 inches.

2. Trace the circle or use the compass to draw a 3½-inch diameter circle on a piece of paper. Use this circle as a pattern by cutting it out and tracing its outline on the foil with the felt tip pen. The center of the circle should be 5 inches down from the top of the rectangle and 5 inches in from the sides.

3. Spoon a ⅛-inch layer of yellow crystals into the circle. Fill the balance of the 10 x 15 inch rectangle with clear crystals to a depth of ⅛ inch.

Lay 4 diamond-shaped mosaics across the diameter of the circle, using Figure 5–7 as your pattern. Fit 3 diamonds in a row above the center and 3 diamonds in a row below it. Then place a row of 2 diamonds above and below, and finally 1 diamond at the top and bottom. You wind up with a large green diamond within the yellow circle.

4. Lay the red mosaic pieces like petals radiating from the center circle. Overlap the rectangles or other red shapes at the edge closest to the center so that they resemble petals (see Fig. 5–6).

Lay the green oblong bar vertically as the stem. Place 2 green circles on either side of the stem to resemble leaves.

Fig. 5-6

Suggested pattern for constructing a mosaic flower.

5. Place the cookie sheet in a 350° oven for 15 minutes. The mosaic pieces should be gummy at that point. Use the handle of the wooden spoon to press down all overlapping pieces to ensure a greater bond. Continue baking until the entire piece looks smooth and glossy, about 25 minutes more.

Remove the pan from the oven and allow your contemporary flower panel to cool.

Combining Mosaics and Lead Cames

USING GEOMETRIC SHAPES IN AN ABSTRACT DESIGN

The colors and shapes of the prebaked mosaic pieces you use in this project will be determined by the abstract "painting" in your mind's eye. I will give the basic procedure, but the design—and therefore the arrangement of pieces and the amount of lead came needed for framing—is up to you. You may even want to make the mosaic shapes with a predetermined picture or specific scene in mind.

MATERIALS	EQUIPMENT
assorted colors and sizes of pre- baked plastic shapes	aluminum foil
	cookie sheet
length of U-channel lead	cutting tool
length of H-channel lead	white glue
	2 1″ x 14″ balsa wood sticks or a T square
	hot mitts
	soldering iron
	60/40 resinous core solder

1. Lay a single length of aluminum foil on the cookie sheet and fold the edges of the foil under the pan on both ends to keep the foil in place.

2. Play with the plastic shapes until you find a design that pleases you. You are not restricted to a square, circle, or triangle; any abstract or irregular design you come up with is fine. But since regular squares or rectangles are slightly more difficult to line up properly, I will give the instructions for that type of "frame".

For a right-angle corner, use a T square or glue 2 wood sticks at right angles to each other on the aluminum foil to serve as a temporary frame for the top and side of your panel.

3. Stretch the lead and cut the top and side lengths of U-channel lead to size and fit them against the wood strips or T square on the cookie sheet.

Fit the corner piece of plastic into the channels of both the top and side pieces of lead as shown in Figure 5–8. Cut the longest adjoining piece of H-channel lead and fit it into place. Continue, working out from the corner until all your pieces of plastic and dividing H-channel lead are in place.

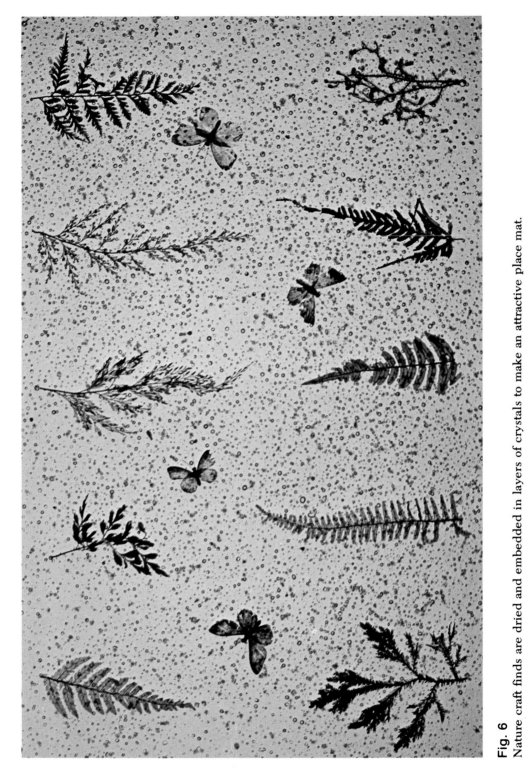

Fig. 6
Nature craft finds are dried and embedded in layers of crystals to make an attractive place mat.

Fig. 7
A distinctive tile sampler in abstract design, easily made using the hammering technique with mosaic pieces.

Fig. 8
The simplest technique of all is used for this mischievous cat—just trace the pattern onto foil and fill with crystals.

Fig. 5–7

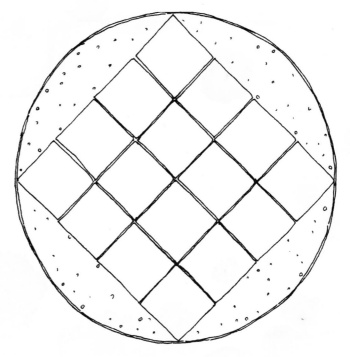

Laying the mosaics in a diamond pattern.

When the design is complete, cut and place the remaining U-channel lengths for the frame.

4. Solder the joints; turn the piece over and solder the joints on the back side. The piece is now complete; further baking is not necessary!

STILL LIFE "PAINTING"

For this project, you'll use leaded shapes within a lead frame to create a cluster of grapes in still life.

MATERIALS	EQUIPMENT
9 round purple mosaics, 1″ to 2″ in diameter	cookie sheet
	aluminum foil
1 rectangular green mosaic ¾″ x 2″	cutting tool
	soldering iron
red and green cooking crystals	60/40 resinous core solder
H- and U-channel lead cames	spoon
	2 1″ x 14″ balsa wood sticks or a T square

1. Cover the cookie sheet with a single length of aluminum foil. Stretch the lead. Cut and shape H-channel lead strips around the 9 purple circles of varying sizes and the green rectangle (Fig. 5–9). Lay the mosaic pieces resembling grapes and stem in the correct arrangement on

Fig. 5-8

Fitting the corner piece into U-channel lead.

the foil. It is not necessary to solder the ends of the lead closed as the melted plastic keeps the lead in place.

Since we have no mosaic shape for the leaf, simply shape the H-channel lead into a leaf form and place it in position on the cookie sheet.

2. Cut 4 pieces of U-channel lead cames using the balsa wood sticks or T square as a guide; place them at right angles around the picture to form a frame (Fig. 5–10).

Solder the frame closed.

3. Fill the spaces within the leaf shape with green cooking crystals. Fill the spaces between grapes and between the grape cluster and the frame with red cooking crystals. Make sure that ample crystals are nudged into the channels of the lead.

4. Place the cookie sheet into the oven at 350°. Bake until all the crystal is smooth and shiny—about 30 to 40 minutes. Remove from the oven and cool.

Fig. 5-9

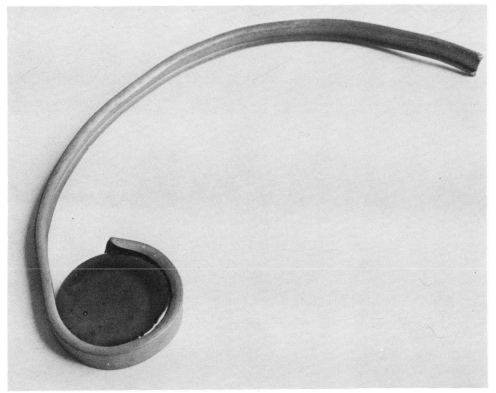

Shaping lead around a mosaic piece.

Fig. 5-10

Using wooden sticks to ensure right angles.

CHAPTER 6

Hammered Designs

HAMMERED designs are created by disturbing or distressing the plastic while it is still in the viscous stage. This can be done while the piece is still in the oven, working with the oven door open and with gloves on your hands. It can also be done in the seconds before the plastic hardens just after removal from the oven, but you have even less time. In either case, you must work quickly. Strands of plastic may lift away on the end of the tool—like strands of mozzarella cheese from a pizza. As soon as the plastic has cooled and hardened, these strands can be broken away.

Hammering produces rippled or textured effects in the plastic, resembling the glass often used in stained glass pieces. The altered surface refracts light in a more exciting way and makes your piece more interesting to look at. Hammering also helps the fusing process if a number of mosaic pieces are being bonded together.

There is no need for special tools: practically anything you can think of (except plastic utensils) can be used. Think of metal and wooden tools in the kitchen drawers or in the garage: slotted spoons, forks, nut crackers, handles, thimbles, spatulas, glasses, hammers, an unsharpened pencil, the eraser end of a pencil with no eraser in it, etc. Any of these things make a good impression. The only precautionary advice I have is be sure you don't hammer so violently as to punch out holes.

TILE SAMPLER

This colorful, distinctive tile is shown in the color section, Figure 7. It can be used as a trivet or a coaster for a small vase, but you may simply want to display it. A number of these might be combined to make a "stained glass" window.

MATERIAL   EQUIPMENT

mosaic shapes or odd pieces of   6″ square baking pan
    plastic in various sizes, shapes,   hot mitts
    and colors   fork, 2-ounce glass, wooden han-
                                         dled utensil

1. Cover the bottom of the baking pan with overlapping pieces of cooking crystal mosaics so that the surface is covered and looks like patchwork (Fig. 6–1). You can build up to 3 layers in some areas for differences in dimension.

2. Place the pan into a 350° oven for approximately 20 minutes. Wearing the hot mitts, open the oven door. With the bottom of the glass, hammer all areas that are 2 or 3 levels high. Don't be neat. Overlapping impressions and bisecting circles make the end result more interesting. With your eye, divide the plastic square into 4 sections. Hammer a section with the open end of the shot glass, rake the fork over one section, prick the plastic with the fork over another, and pound with the handle over the last section (Fig. 6–2).

3. Remove the pan from the oven and allow the plastic to cool for about 20 minutes before turning it out of the pan. Your tile sampler is complete.

Fig. 6–1

Cover the bottom of the pan with mosaics or prebaked plastic pieces.

Fig. 6-2

Hammer and disturb the surface of the hot plastic.

MEDALLIONS AND PENDANTS

The designs of medallions are really suggested by the mosaic pieces themselves. Several attractive configurations are shown in Figure 5, color section.

MATERIALS	EQUIPMENT
mosaic pieces in assorted sizes, shapes, and colors	cookie sheet
cord	aluminum foil
	hammering tools
	hot mitts
	cotton gloves
	skewer
	scissors
	ruler

1. Cover the cookie sheet with 4 separate pieces of aluminum foil, each large enough to contain 1 design.

On each foil square, arrange any 3 mosaic pieces so that they overlap at the center (Fig. 6–3). The pieces may be the same color or 3 different colors.

2. Place the cookie sheet into a 350° oven for about 20 minutes. Open the oven door. With the gloves on your hands and the tools within easy reach, pound and hammer the mosaic pieces so that each of the sets of 3 mosaics is firmly fused.

Remove the cookie sheet from the oven and allow the pieces to cool for about 15 minutes.

Fig. 6–3

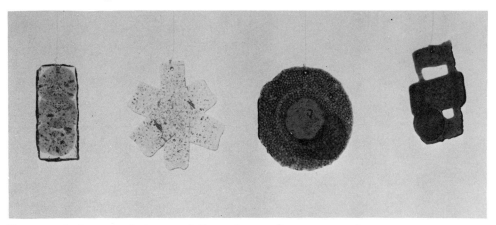

Hammered pieces made into medallions for jewelry or sun catchers.

3. Heat the skewer over an open flame and pierce a hole through the top of each medallion or pendant.

Thread the cord (or chain or leather thong) through the holes. Hang the pieces in a window, on a Christmas tree, or around your neck!

CHAPTER 7

Practical Household Projects

EVERYTHING I have discussed up to this point should be considered useful information or technique. While you have been using individual techniques to produce finished products, I would like to encourage you to look for opportunities to combine several methods in one project. Put your imagination to work, adding and combining what you already know with the projects that follow. For example, you can embed things in kitchen molds; you can hammer leaded plastic; you can frame an aluminum foil drawing with U-channel lead cames; and turn mosaic pieces into jewelry beads. If you get a new idea, try it! That's one of the most exciting aspects of this craft.

As you have already seen, cooking crystals can be used to make functional objects as well as purely decorative ones. The plastic is washable, durable, fadeproof, and scratch resistant. It is not heat resistant, however, so it must never come in direct contact with flame or with extreme heat. The heat of a cigarette being extinguished is enough to mar the plastic, thus eliminating its use in ashtrays, with the exception described later in this chapter. Cooking crystals can be used to make trivets if you exercise the same amount of care as you would ordinarily use with plastic topped kitchen counters—hot, but not too hot!

MAKING USEFUL TRAYS

Trays are basically cooking crystals—with or without embedments—poured into a large, flat mold. Jelly roll, roasting, and pizza pans are obvious choices, depending on the shape you want. Hammering the surface of a tray is not practical, as it makes the surface uneven. The crystals can range from ⅛ to ½ inch in thickness. Holes can be pierced or drilled in the plastic after baking for the addition of handles if you want them.

88

ORANGE SWIRL TRAY

I made the tray shown in Figure 7–1 with swirls of orange and transparent crystals. You may want to vary the color scheme to match your breakfast china.

MATERIALS	EQUIPMENT
¼ lb. orange cooking crystals	new or clean 12″ pizza pan
¼ lb. clear cooking crystals	spoon
4 fiber washers	tweezers
2 handles with screws	hot mitts
	metal knitting needle
	screw driver
	pen or pencil

Fig. 7–1

Finished orange swirl tray with handles.

1. Spoon the orange crystals directly into the bottom of the pizza pan. Use your index finger to push the crystals into an off-center spiral as shown in Figure 7–2. The crystals should be about ⅛-inch deep.

Using a spoon, carefully fill the spaces between the orange swirls with clear crystals. Use the tweezers to remove any orange crystals that might fall into the transparent ones.

2. Carefully place the pan into a 350° oven for approximately 45 minutes or until the surface is smooth and shiny.

Remove the pan from the oven and allow it to cool for about 30 minutes. Turn the tray out and replace it upside down in the pan. Return it to the 350° oven for an additional 5 minutes to remove any rough or uneven edges.

Remove the pan from the oven and allow it to cool once again; turn the tray out of the pan. You could, of course, use it without the handles, but adding them makes a more useful tray.

3. Place the handles in position on either side of the tray (see Fig. 7–1). On the back side, mark the plastic with a pen or pencil to show the location of the holes in the handles. Heat the knitting needle and pierce holes through the plastic at the locations marked. Place the fiber washers against the bottom of the tray and screw the handles into place.

Fig. 7-2

Making the spiral design.

PICTURE FRAME TRAY

In Chapter 2 you learned that melting plastic adheres to the material surrounding it. This perfectly simple method used with an empty wooden picture frame produces the handsome contemporary tray shown in the color section, Figure 11. Taking the motif of the frame as a cue, the overall design of the plastic can be modern, traditional, rustic, period—you can easily modify the instructions for any "flavor" picture you want.

MATERIALS	EQUIPMENT
a simple black 11″ x 14″ frame	cookie sheet
¼ lb. clear cooking crystals	aluminum foil
1 oz. each of red, orange, yellow,	hot mitts
green, pink, and purple crystals	spoon
	tweezers
	paper
	ruler
	scissors
	felt tip pen

1. Measure off the shapes you want on paper and cut them out; I used 6 equal 3-inch squares for the design shown in Figure 7–3; you might like to try a variety of geometric shapes and sizes.

2. Cover the cookie sheet with a length of aluminum foil and lay the empty picture frame on it, with the front facing you. Arrange the paper cutouts within the frame to get the design you want. Overlap some corners so that 2 colors of crystals will be superimposed (see Fig. 7–3).

Trace the outlines of the shapes onto the foil with a felt tip pen, removing the cutouts as you do so.

3. Spoon the crystals, one color at a time, into each of the shapes on the foil. The depth of the crystals should match the height of the frame; that is, where a picture would be if you were framing it. Try to get the overlapping colors the same depth as the areas with only one color.

Spoon the clear crystal background into the remaining spaces. Use the tweezers to remove any stray granules from the wrong color areas.

4. Place the cookie sheet into the oven at 350° for approximately 45 minutes or until the surface is smooth and shiny.

Remove the cookie sheet from the oven and allow the tray to cool for approximately 30 minutes. The molten crystals will have adhered to the picture frame and will be sturdy enough to act as a very serviceable tray. It could also be a very attractive, neatly framed picture.

Making Coasters

Coasters are extremely simple to make using muffin tins, toy baking pans, or shapes drawn on aluminum foil. There are no rigid rules—anything goes! This is a good project for young children, and the important

Fig. 7-3

An empty frame is placed right side up on foil, and the painting designed with cutouts.

part is to make the coaster designs interesting. Don't be afraid to experiment: combine colors; embed anything! You have nothing to lose except a few grains of crystal and some trivia!

MUFFIN TIN COASTERS

I have previously discussed the use of muffin tins as suitable molds. They are an easy, fast, and efficient method of turning out 6, 8, or 12

Fig. 7–4

Filling muffin tins to make coasters.

coasters in a short period of time. Coasters do not have to be identical to make a lovely set, but you'll want to plan some degree of sameness in the colors used or in the complexity of the designs.

MATERIAL	EQUIPMENT
8 ounces cooking crystals	muffin tin
	hot mitts
	aluminum foil
	cookie sheet

1. Spoon the crystals into each compartment of the muffin tin to a depth of ⅛ to ¼ inch (Fig. 7–4). Add any embedment or variation in colors that you want.

2. Place the muffin tin in a 350° oven for approximately 20 to 30 minutes, until the crystals are smooth and shiny.

Remove the tin from the oven and allow it to cool for 15 to 20 minutes before turning the coasters out. Then turn them upside down on a foil-covered cookie sheet (Fig. 7–5) and return them to the oven for 5 minutes. When thoroughly cooled, the coasters are ready to use.

Fig. 7-5

Returning the discs to the oven to smooth all edges.

MADCAP COASTERS

You can make square or odd-shaped coasters by drawing the outline with a felt tip pen or crayon on a foil-covered cookie sheet. There will be a slight degree of spreading as the crystals melt, but it is never enough to alter your design or to constitute a problem. Try octagonals, "blob" shapes, anything—just don't draw them too close together.

MATERIALS	EQUIPMENT
cooking crystals	cookie sheet
selected embedment (optional)	aluminum foil
	felt tip pen
	paper
	scissors
	spoon
	tweezers
	hot mitt

1. Cover the cookie sheet with a length of aluminum foil. Make a paper pattern of the shape you selected, cut it out, then trace and retrace it on the foil: you should be able to make 6 to 8 coasters in one baking.

2. Spoon crystals into each of the shapes to a depth of no more than ¼ inch. If you are adding embedment, be sure it is completely covered with crystals.

3. Place the cookie sheet into a 350° oven for approximately 30 minutes, depending on the depth of the crystals. When the coasters look smooth and shiny (Fig. 7–6), remove the cookie sheet from the oven and allow them to cool for about 20 minutes before peeling them off the foil.

MAKING BOWLS AND AN ASHTRAY

Until this point, you have never attempted to use the crystals in other than a flat, or two-dimensional, shape. Yet bowls and dishes are extremely easy to make and turn out quite beautifully (see color section, Fig. 12). Basically, items in this category require two baking periods: the first to fuse the crystals in the usual manner, and the second to alter the flat disc into a bowl or dish with curved or flared sides. You will want to experiment with making bowls from various sizes of discs to achieve varying depths or flares.

Fig. 7–6

Square coasters; make any shapes you'd like.

Fig. 7-7

Design is planned around the outside edges of the bowl.

BASIC BOWL

MATERIALS	EQUIPMENT
½ lb. cooking crystals	12″ pizza pan
embedments such as leaves and butterflies or glass gems (optional)	metal or Pyrex bowl with 5″ base hot mitts

1. Pour a layer of crystals into the bottom of the pizza pan. If you are using embedments, sandwich them between layers of crystals. Do not place any embedments within a 4-inch diameter at the center of the pan (Fig. 7-7), as this will be the bottom of the finished bowl and when the crystals drape during the second baking, embedments could be exposed to oven heat. The depth of the crystals should be between ⅛ and ¼ inch. Smooth them out so they are as level as possible.

2. Place the pizza pan into a 350° oven and bake until the plastic looks smooth and glossy—about 45 minutes.

Remove the pan from the oven and allow it to cool for 30 minutes before removing the plastic disc from the pan.

3. Place the mixing bowl upside down on the pizza pan. Center the plastic disc on the bottom of the inverted bowl so that it is balanced as shown in Figure 7-8.

Fig. 7–8

Place the disc over the bottom of an inverted bowl.

Carefully place the 3-tiered project into the oven at 350°. As the heat softens the plastic, the area extending beyond the bottom of the mixing bowl droops down and gracefully forms the contours of your new bowl. This does not take a long time: check progress at the end of 5 minutes. When it looks "right," remove everything from the oven and allow the plastic to cool again for about 20 minutes. When thoroughly cooled, it can be easily lifted off the mixing bowl. The plastic bowl retains its shape once it has hardened.

HAND-SHAPED BOWL

Instead of using a bowl to mold this, you'll shape the contours by hand. Naturally, you can use whatever colors, designs, or embedments you choose.

MATERIAL   EQUIPMENT

cooking crystals   pie pan
                                                           tin can
                                                           cotton gloves
                                                           hot mitts

1. Pour a ⅛- to ¼-inch layer of crystals on the bottom of the pie pan in whatever design you'd like.

2. Place the pan into a 350° oven for approximately 30 minutes or until the crystal is smooth and glossy. Remove the pan from the oven and allow it to cool.

Remove the disc from the pan. Stand the tin can upright in the center of the pan and balance the disc on top of the tin can. Place all 3 pieces carefully into the 350° oven.

Fig. 7–9

Shaping a bowl over a tin can.

3. After approximately 2 minutes, place the hot mitts or cotton gloves on your hands. Open the oven door and shape the softened disc downwards into the form you like (Fig. 7–9).

Remove everything from the oven and allow it to cool for about 20 minutes before removing the bowl from the can.

EXCEPTION-TO-THE-RULE BOWL

A shallow bowl can be made in one step by using aluminum foil as your mold. The foil allows you to make a free-form bowl by cupping and creasing the foil so that it contains the crystals during the baking process. The foil mold must be shallow enough so that the unbaked crystals cling to the contour of the sides without falling to the bottom of the mold.

MATERIALS	EQUIPMENT
cooking crystals	12″ square of heavy duty foil
	baking pan
	spoon
	hot mitts

Fig. 7–10

A free-form aluminum foil bowl is filled with crystals.

1. Bend up the sides of the foil so that the base is in any free-form shape you like, but with no side less than 1 inch high.

Crease all the folds as tightly as possible so that the foil cannot be trapped within the melted plastic. Foil trapped in this manner is difficult, and sometimes impossible, to remove.

2. Place the foil mold on a baking pan, just for ease in handling. Spoon the crystals into the foil mold, using the back of the spoon to push the crystals up the sides as far as they will go without falling back (Fig. 7–10). The crystals on the bottom of the mold should be about ⅛-inch deep; the sides will be somewhat thinner.

3. Place the pan into a 350° oven and bake about 30 minutes or until the plastic is smooth and glossy.

Remove the pan from the oven. Let the bowl cool for about 20 minutes before peeling the aluminum foil away.

ASHTRAY

As I mentioned before, the heat of a cigarette being snuffed out against the plastic is enough to mar the surface. It will not cause the plastic to go up in flames, but it will spoil its appearance. Therefore, I devised the following method, encasing a glass ashtray in a cooking crystal shell.

MATERIALS	EQUIPMENT
½ lb. of cooking crystals	pie pan
glass ashtray	6″ tart mold
	tin can
	cotton gloves
	hot mitts
	cement glue

1. Fill the tart mold with crystals to a depth of ⅛ to ¼ inch in the design of your choice. Hammered mosaic pieces work well in this project.

2. Place the pan into a 350° oven for approximately 30 minutes or until the crystals are glossy and smooth.

Remove the pan from the oven and allow to cool for about 20 minutes before turning the disc out of the pan.

3. Stand the tin can upright in the center of the pie pan; place the glass ashtray upside down on top of the can; center the plastic disc on top of the ashtray (Fig. 7–11). Carefully place the 3-tiered project into the 350° oven.

Place the gloves or mitts on your hands and, as soon as the plastic disc begins to droop, open the oven door. Mold and bend the edges of the plastic around the edge of the glass ashtray so that the ashtray is captured within the plastic shell.

Fig. 7-11

The plastic disc is placed over the bottom of a glass ashtray.

4. Remove the pieces from the oven and allow to cool for about 20 minutes. When you remove the ashtray and set it right side up, the glass inside is exposed. It is thus safe for use and the plastic design can be seen through it. If the plastic is not firmly attached to the ashtray, apply a few drops of cement glue.

COMBINING COOKING CRYSTALS WITH OTHER CRAFTS

The techniques you have already learned can be used in conjunction with other crafts to produce some really marvelous distinctive and useful items. Try the next two projects for a sampling, then begin to think how you can combine other familiar handicrafts with the techniques you've learned working with cooking crystals—with a vivid imagination, you can probably think of literally hundreds of projects for ornamental or practical items combining two or more crafts.

The first project in this section combines bread dough and crystals to make a very practical trivet; if you find that you enjoy working with dough craft, Chilton's Basic Crafts Series includes a book on the myriad techniques used to *Start off in Dough Craft*.

A hanging planter is the next project, combining a cooking crystal "bowl" with pop-top hanging apparatus. The project includes instructions for making chains and flowers, but to learn more about making fantastic garments and household projects, get *Pop-Topping*! See the inside back cover or flap for a complete listing of books on crafts that are great individually or in combination with COOKING CRYSTAL CRAFT.

CRYSTAL DOUGH CRAFT TRIVET

Since bread dough and cooking crystals must both be baked, I combined them to make a safe, but not edible, trivet that can be used on the table or near the stove. See the photograph, Figure 10, in the color section.

The dough can be colored with powdered or liquid tempera paint or food coloring before baking. Black tempera will give you the leaded stained glass effect; other colors can match your table setting; or the natural dough, undyed, bakes to a delicious crusty brown.

The dough becomes soggy even if it's sprayed with acrylic, so don't wash the trivet or use it near water.

MATERIALS	EQUIPMENT
4 cups flour	mixing bowl
1 cup salt	rolling pin
2 cups water	knife
powdered or liquid tempera or	12″ pizza pan
food coloring (optional)	spatula
1 tsp. cooking oil	spoon
1 lb. cooking crystals	clear acrylic spray

1. Combine the flour, salt, and water in a mixing bowl. Add the tempera or food coloring, if desired, to the shade you wish. Mix until it is a soft, workable dough. Turn the dough onto a floured work surface and roll it out to a thickness of one inch with a lightly floured rolling pin.

2. Slice off a piece of dough and roll it between the palms of your hands until you get a single strand about ½-inch thick and 5 or 6 inches long as shown in Figure 7–12. Bring the ends of the strand together to make a loop, closing the loop by dipping your fingers in water and wetting the ends to make a smooth seam. Lay the loop on a lightly greased pizza pan next to the edge.

Continue making loops, laying them around the circumference of the pan. Use water to connect each loop to the ones adjoining it. Continue making inner rows of loops until the entire pan is covered with them (Fig.

Fig. 7–12

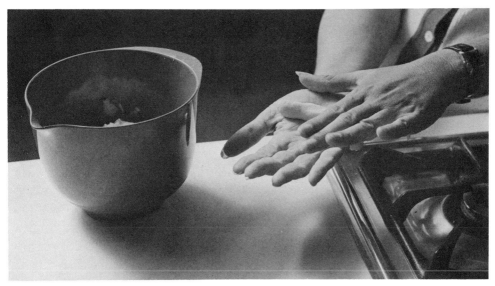

Rolling a length of bread dough for a loop.

Fig. 7–13

Spooning crystals into bread dough loops for the trivet.

7–13). The loops should not be perfect circles; they are more attractive if they are squeezed and stretched into the existing spaces.

3. Spoon cooking crystals about ¼-inch thick into each loop, using one color of crystals or several. Don't fill the spaces between the loops.

4. Set the oven temperature at 400° instead of the usual 350°. The dough acts as an insulator, and at the lower temperature the crystals fuse but don't get to the glossy stage during the same amount of time that the dough takes to achieve a well-baked look. This generally takes about 45 minutes. However, if you have colored the dough black or some other dark color, you can continue baking until the crystals acquire the look you want.

5. Remove the pan from the oven and allow it to cool about 30 minutes. To make sure you don't break the bread dough while removing it from the pan, place the spatula underneath the trivet to free any dough that might have stuck to the pan.

Spray the trivet with clear acrylic for protection against moisture and as a reminder that the dough is not edible. It is now ready for use.

POP-TOPPING A HANGING PLANTER

You'll use aluminum pop-tops—the ring and tab closures from beverage cans—to make the hanging apparatus that turns a cooking crystal bowl into a hanging planter! There are a number of different types of pop-tops, varying by beverage brand: it does not matter which kind you use, but they should all be identical. As you collect them near almost any concession stand at a park or sports arena where the ground is littered with them, you'll also be doing your bit for ecology!

As you collect your pop-tops, wash them in hot soapy water with a stiff-bristled brush; then dry and sort them. When you have accumulated 103 pop-tops of the same type, you're ready to go!

To make the cooking crystal bowl shape, you'll need a metal or ovenproof glass bowl 3 inches in diameter across the bottom and 7 inches in diameter at the top—a squat, rounded shape. If you have anything suitable that comes close, use it; if you do not have a bowl answering this description, put the crystal disc on top of a can 3 inches in diameter. Then, when the molten crystals begin to drape down over the can, proceed as you did for the Hand-Shaped Bowl project: allow the can to determine the bottom of the bowl, and working quickly with the viscous plastic, flare the rim of the bowl outward, "eyeballing" an approximate 7-inch diameter as you work.

MATERIALS	EQUIPMENT
103 pop-tops, all alike	12″ pizza pan
½ lb. cooking crystals, any color	tureen or mixing bowl: 7″ diameter
1½″ diameter heavy metal ring	top, 3″ diameter bottom
	pliers
	work gloves
	hot mitts

1. To begin making your pop-top chains, pick up a single pop-top in your left hand, holding it firmly by the ring; place a second pop-top ring onto the tab of the first as illustrated in Figure 7–14.

Fold the tab of the first pop-top up and through the ring as shown in Figure 7–15, pressing the tab down firmly in back. You now have a 2-link chain. Add each pop-top in the same manner, working until the chain is 16 links long. Do not bind the rings tightly in the tabs: you want these hanging chains to be flexible.

Make 5 more chains, each 16 links long. Let the loose tabs at the end of each chain dangle freely.

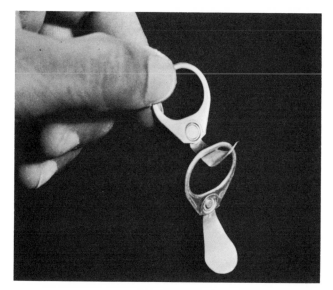

Fig. 7-14

Hold the first pop-top as shown, placing a second one on the tab. *(From Pop-Topping! by Pop-Top Terp with Kenneth Patton, copyright © 1975 by the author, reprinted with permission of Chilton Book Company, Radnor, Pa.)*

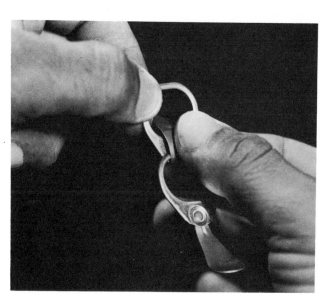

Fig. 7-15

Fold the tab of the first pop-top up through the ring. Press it flat in back with your forefinger. *(From Pop-Topping! by Pop-Top Terp with Kenneth Patton, copyright © 1975 by the author, reprinted with permission of Chilton Book Company, Radnor, Pa.)*

2. You have 7 pop-tops left and will use these to make a pop-top flower for the center bottom of the hanger. Take 1 pop-top and *break the tab off of it:* this ring is the center ring of your flower.

Now take a whole pop-top and slip the center ring over its tab as shown in Figure 7–16: fold the tab through the ring at exactly the point where you broke the tab off this ring and press the tab down firmly in back, as you did when adding links to a chain. Your flower now has a single petal.

Add 2 additional pop-tops to the center ring at the right of the first petal; then add 2 more to the left of this first petal—your flower will now look exactly like the one in Figure 7–17. The sixth and last petal must be

Fig. 7–16

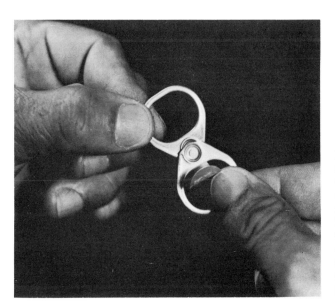

Place the center ring of the flower onto the tab of the whole pop-top. Fold the tab through the ring, pressing it flat in back. (*From Pop-Topping! by Pop-Top Terp with Kenneth Patton, copyright © 1975 by the author, reprinted with permission of Chilton Book Company, Radnor, Pa.*)

Fig. 7–17

Five petals have been added to the flower. Add your last petal on the flat part of the center ring. (*From Pop-Topping! by Pop-Top Terp with Kenneth Patton, copyright © 1975 by the author, reprinted with permission of Chilton Book Company, Radnor, Pa.*)

added to the flat part of the ring at the top—if you put an earlier petal on this portion of the ring, the flower goes awry.

3. Now pick up 1 of the chains you made in step 1: fold the loose tab at the end of that chain through a single petal of your pop-top flower. Firmly press the tab through the petal ring and press it down in back.

Fold the free tab at the end of each of your 5 remaining chains through 1 of the flower petals. If you lay it out flat on your work surface, you now have a flower center with 6 pop-top chains radiating outward, similar to the spokes of a wheel.

4. Fill the pizza pan with cooking crystals to a depth of ⅛ inch and place it in a 350° oven for approximately 30 minutes. When the crystals look smooth and glossy, remove the pan from the oven and allow it to cool thoroughly.

5. Turn the crystal disc out of the pan; invert your bowl or can on the pan and center the crystal disc on top. Place the 3-tiered project into a 350° oven until the crystals again become molten and drape down over the sides of the bowl.

If you are using a bowl roughly the shape of the one I described, go on to step 6. If you placed the disc over a can, you now must open the oven door and quickly work the plastic into a rounded planter shape.

6. When the crystal disc has draped down and conformed to the shape of the bowl, gather up the pop-top chains firmly in your gloved left hand. Pull out the shelf, but do not remove the project from the oven. Working as quickly as you can, take the pop-top flower in your right hand and place it in the exact center of the bottom of the bowl, still holding the chains firmly in your left hand.

Now separate a *single chain* with your right hand and press it into the plastic, again like a spoke radiating from the flower center. Leave the chain links that extend beyond the bowl's rim lay loose on the pan underneath. Separating 1 chain at a time, press each one into the plastic, dividing the bowl into 6 equal parts and allowing excess chain links to flop down on the pan.

Give the whole thing the once-over, making sure the pop-tops are pressed firmly into the plastic (but not embedded) before you remove the project from the oven. Allow it to cool thoroughly, then remove your planter and turn it right side up.

Slightly separate the closure on a heavy metal ring with your pliers; slip the end rings of all 6 chains through the opening and close the metal ring tightly with your pliers. Now plant your very favorite wild thing in the planter and hang it from a sturdy hook or nail.

CHAPTER 8

Creative Jewelry

THE most difficult part of making jewelry with cooking crystals is knowing the names of the findings you'll need to buy. In other words, *it's easy*! Your essential tools are: needle-nose pliers with which to open and close wire loops; and clear, waterproof glue (such as Dow Corning Glass Adhesive® or Wilhold Jewelry Cement®) to fasten anything else.

JEWELRY FINDINGS

First I'll list the names of the various jewelry findings and describe their functions. An assortment of the ones most frequently used is shown in Figure 8–1. The findings are relatively inexpensive and are available in gold or silver color at just about every hobby store or craft center. If you need a catalog see Sources of Supply.

Jump Rings. Circles or loops of wire with a single cut or opening in them, jump rings are the joiners. You fasten one section of your jewelry to another using the jump ring as the connector. Simply open or separate the cut in the wire with pliers, insert another jump ring, a clasp, or a chain link (Fig. 8–2). Then you close the jump ring with the pliers and the two pieces are permanently connected. Jump rings come in various sizes, but the size is only critical in that it be large enough to hold the links or loops you are connecting.

Clasps. These opening and closing mechanisms allow you to wear a chain around your neck that won't fit over your head or a chain around your wrist that won't fit over your hand. Clasps come in two sections—one for each end of the chain making up the necklace or bracelet. They are available with safety catches or with simple hooks and rings (left center, Fig. 8–1); the kind you buy will depend upon the value of the jewelry you make.

Fig. 8–1

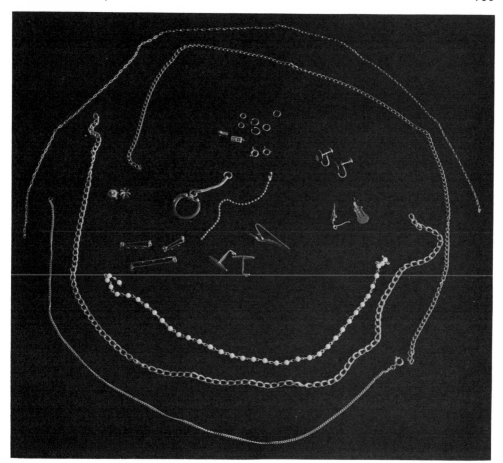

Jewelry findings: various styles of chains make up the outside circle. In the inside circle, *clockwise from top,* findings are: button earrings, drop or loop earrings, tie tack, cuff links, brooches or pins, bell cap, key chains, clasps and jump rings.

Chains. Jewelry chains can be purchased by the foot or yard in many different styles (see Fig. 8–1). For a necklace, you'll need 18-, 27-, or 36-inch lengths, depending on the size of the pendant and its style. You should have about 7 to 8 inches of chain for a bracelet. Since chains are sold by the length, determine the amount you need before buying.

Bell Caps. These are little filigreed cups of soft metal with loops on the tops of the closed ends (bottom center, Fig. 8–1). Baked cooking crystal beads or trinkets are glued into the open end of the cup while the loop is joined to the chain by means of a jump ring.

Pin Clasps. The pin for attaching the brooch to a garment is attached to a flat metal bar (lower center, Fig. 8–1). Your ornament is attached to the face of the bar with glue.

Earring Findings. You can buy wires for pierced ears; you can buy clip-on or screw-on styles for unpierced ears (upper center, Fig. 8–1). Earring findings are available with loops for drop earrings and with metal

Fig. 8–2

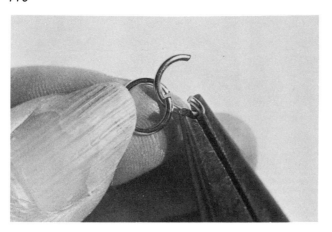

Connecting jump rings to-
gether with pliers.

discs for button styles. Make sure the findings meet all your requirements
when you buy them.

Cuff Links and Tie Tacks. These fastenings have a small metal disc to
which you glue the ornament (center right, Fig. 8–1).

Key Rings. There are two types of key ring holders (at center, Fig.
8–1). The least expensive is a short length of chain that looks like a row of
little balls. The chain opens and closes with a clasp. Both the ornament
and the keys are attached to the chain. The more expensive key chain
(about 15¢) has a circle for holding keys at one end of the chain and a small
loop at the other end for attaching the ornament.

MAKING JEWELRY WITH MOLDED ORNAMENTS

Cooking crystals baked in lead strips, candy, tart, or petit fours molds,
cookie cutters, or children's toy baking pans are all small enough to be
worn as pendants. Objects made from candy molds and miniature
Frame-Ups are small enough to be used as earrings and charms. Some
delightful examples of mold-made jewelry are shown in the color section,
Figure 9.

Pendants, earrings, charm bracelets, brooches, cuff links, tie clasps, or
key chains are all made in basically the same way. Only the number of
objects and the findings used vary. Keeping this in mind, you know that
you can make a bracelet from my directions for a pendant, merely by
changing the length of the chain and the number of objects hanging from
it. While reading the directions for any one piece of jewelry, look for new
possibilities and new directions to explore in jewelry projects of your own
creation.

It is not necessary to always use a chain for a necklace or bracelet. For
reasons of economy, aesthetics, or expediency, you may wish to substitute
ribbon, leather thongs, macrame cord, braid, yarn, or string. Anything is
right if you say it is.

PENDANT

Before you begin the instructions here for assembling the pendant necklace, design and make your own pendant ornament. You may want to make one of the framed adornments in Chapter 2, or a pendant from one of the small molds according to the techniques you learned in Chapter 3.

MATERIALS	EQUIPMENT
plastic ornament	metal skewer or knitting needle
1 yd. of jewelry chain	needle-nose pliers
2 large jump rings	hot mitts
clasp (optional)	

1. With a heated skewer or knitting needle, pierce a hole through the top of the baked plastic object.
2. Open each jump ring by holding it between your thumb and forefinger with one hand while pushing one end of the circle back with the pliers held in the other hand (see Fig. 8–2).

Slip the ornament onto an opened jump ring. With the pliers, close the jump ring so that it is a closed circle again.
3. Fold the length of chain in half to find the center link. Slip another opened jump ring through the link of the chain that is most nearly in the center, then slip it through the jump ring that is attached to the ornament. Use the pliers to close the jump ring tightly.
4. If you want to attach a clasp, open the link at each end of the chain with your pliers. Attach half of the clasp to each end of the chain. Squeeze the links closed again with the pliers to secure the clasp halves. Open and close the clasp as often as you like; the pieces are permanently attached.

If the chain is long enough to go over your head easily, you may not want to use a clasp. Just open *one* of the end links with your pliers, slip the closed link from the other end of the chain into the open link, and use the pliers to close the link again. The chain will then be one continuous loop.

DROP EARRINGS

Again, you'll make the ornaments before starting to assemble the earrings. In addition to using ornaments cast in molds, you can also hammer out the circles and loops that are popular for drop earrings.

MATERIALS	EQUIPMENT
2 plastic ornaments	skewer
1 pair drop earring findings	hot mitts
4 jump rings	pliers

1. With the heated skewer, pierce a hole through the top center of both ornaments.

2. Open the jump rings with the pliers and insert an ornament onto 2 of your jump rings. Attach a second jump ring to each of the first ones. Before closing the second jump rings, insert the loop at the bottom of the findings onto them. Thus, the loop of each finding holds 2 jump rings and 1 ornament. Make sure the ornament hangs with its front side facing outward.

Close the jump rings with the pliers and the earrings are ready to wear.

BUTTON EARRINGS, CUFF LINKS, TIE TACKS, AND BROOCHES

The method is basically the same for assembling button earrings, cuff links, tie tacks, and brooches or pins. The findings for jewelry in this category all have a facet to which the ornament is glued.

When designing your "jewels" for these findings, be sure they are appropriate in size and shape. All you need to complete the task is a transparent glue made for use with metal and plastic—then, with ornaments and findings in hand, simply follow the application and drying instructions on the tube of glue.

CHARM BRACELET

For a charm bracelet to look "right," the charms must be evenly spaced along the length of the chain. For example, if you have only one charm, you should place it midway on the chain. I suggest that you attach the clasp (half at each end of the chain) before attaching the charms. It is then easier to determine the proper spacing, so you can avoid having a sparse look along the length of the bracelet with too many charms bunched around the clasp.

If you use a 7- or 8-inch chain (the proper length for most people), you will find the following guides for charm placement convenient.

> *A 7-inch chain with:*
> 2 charms—place both 2¼″ in from the ends;
> 3 charms—place 1 in the center, with 1 positioned 2½″
>   in from each end;
> 4 charms—place a charm 1½″ from each end, the others
>   1⅝″ toward the center;
> 5 charms—place a charm ½″ from each end, additional 3 charms
>   every 1½″;
> 6 charms—place a charm 1″ from each end, additional 4
>   placed every 1″;
> 7 charms—place a charm ½″ from each end, additional 5 every
>   1″.

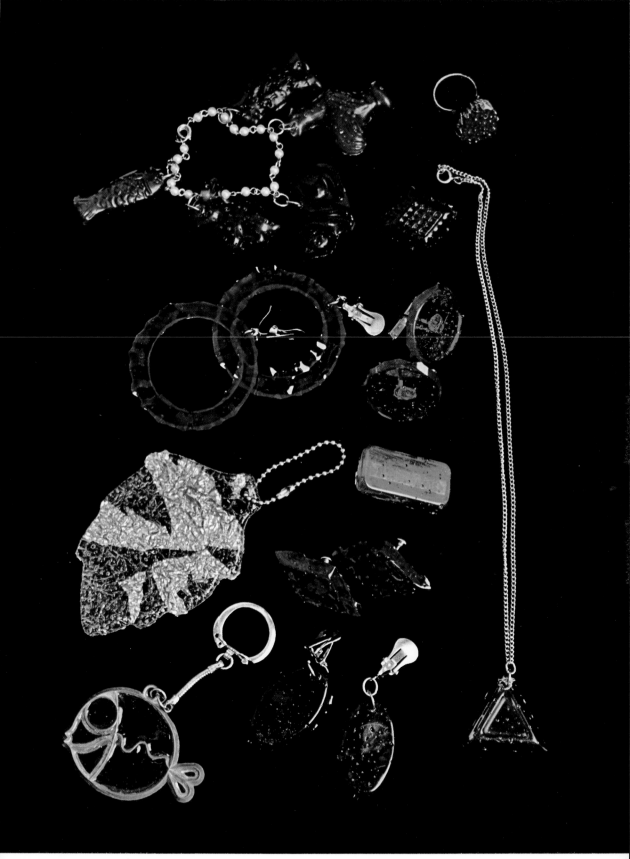

Fig. 9
A small sampling of the beautiful jewelry you can make
with tiny molded crystals ornaments and findings.

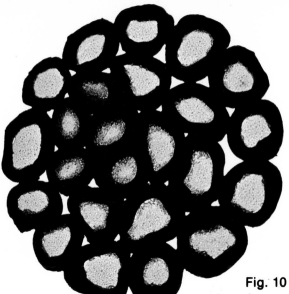

Fig. 10
A marvelous trivet, combining dough craft and cooking crystal craft!

Fig. 11
An ordinary picture frame filled with a crystal design is transformed in the oven into a remarkable and useful tray.

An 8-inch chain with:

> 2 charms—place both 2¾″ from the ends;
>
> 3 charms—place 1 in the center, others 1½″ in from the ends;
>
> 4 charms—place a charm 2″ in from each end, others 2″ toward the center;
>
> 5 charms—place a charm 1″ in from each end, additional 3 every 1½″;
>
> 6 charms—place a charm ⅞″ from each end, additional 4 placed every 1¼″;
>
> 7 charms—place a charm 1″ from each end, additional 5 every 1″;
>
> 8 charms—place a charm ½″ from each end, additional 6 every 1″.

MATERIALS	EQUIPMENT
7″ or 8″ length of chain	pliers
clasp	skewer
1 to 8 charms	hot mitts
twice as many jump rings as charms (2 to 16)	ruler

1. Use a hot skewer to puncture a hole in the top of each ornament.

2. Use the pliers to open each jump ring. Slip a jump ring through the hole in each ornament, but do not close the jump rings.

3. Separate the halves of the clasp. Use pliers to open the jump rings attached to the ends of each of the clasp halves. Slip the last link of each end of the chain onto the opened rings and use the pliers to close the rings.

4. Lay the chain along the length of a ruler and refer to the preceding section to determine where you want your charms.

Slip an *unattached jump ring* through each link that is to hold a charm. Close each jump ring with the pliers as you attach it.

5. Slip the open jump ring attached to a charm through a closed jump ring attached to the chain. Close the second jump ring with the pliers. Continue in this fashion until all the charms are attached to the chain.

KEY CHAINS

Select either style of key ring finding and make an ornament suitable for it.

MATERIALS	EQUIPMENT
ornament	skewer
key chain	hot mitt
jump ring	pliers

1. If the ornament does not have a hole at the top, puncture the ornament at the top center with a hot skewer.

2. Open the jump ring with pliers and slip the end of the jump ring through the hole in the ornament. Do not close the jump ring yet.

3. If the key chain is the simple ball link type, just place the jump ring on the chain at any point. Use the pliers to close the jump ring.

If the key chain has a clasped circle at one end, it has a jump ring attached to the other. Slip the jump ring with the ornament on it through the attached jump ring. Use the pliers to close the second jump ring tightly.

RINGS

Ring findings, which have cupped or depressed centers, can be filled with cooking crystals and baked. The crystals, of course, melt and you then have a "wall to wall" jewel permanently set into the finding. (If you have a problem locating ring findings of this description see the Source of Supply listing.)

MATERIALS	EQUIPMENT
ring finding	clay or dough
1 tablespoon cooking crystals	baking pan
	hot mitts

1. Roll a lump of clay or dough into a ball about 2 inches in diameter. Set the ball on the baking pan so that the bottom of it is flattened against the surface of the pan.

2. Insert the back of the ring finding into the lump of clay. The cup or depression should be exposed and should be resting on the surface of the clay. Adjust the position of the ring so that the cup is perfectly level.

3. Fill the cup with cooking crystals as shown in Figure 8–3. Heap the crystals in the center to allow for shrinkage during the baking process.

4. Place the pan into a 350° oven and bake until the crystals have fused, about 15 minutes.

Remove the pan from the oven and allow the ring to cool for about 15 minutes before removing the ring from the clay. It may pull right out, or you may need to crack the clay if it hardened from the heat.

Using Beads Made From Mosaic Pieces

Beads are made in the 2-part mosaic method. You must first know what size beads you'll need, how many of them, and what colors. Don't try to make them too dainty; larger ones are easier to work with. The diameter should be a minimum of ¾ inch, the minimum length about the same.

For drop earrings, you may need 2 or 4 beads. For a necklace, you may want up to 40; for a medallion, you may need only 6.

Fig. 8–3

Using clay to balance ring
finding filled with crystals.

An assortment of jewelry made from mosaic beads is shown in Figure
8–4.

There is no limit to the lovely accents you can make once you've
mastered this basic method of making the beads.

MAKING THE BEADS

MATERIAL	EQUIPMENT
cooking crystals in assorted colors	cookie sheet
	aluminum foil
	scoring or cutting tools
	hot mitts
	cotton gloves
	metal knitting needle, size 9

1. Spread a ⅛-inch layer of cooking crystals on a foil-covered cookie
sheet.

Bake the crystals at 350° until they are smooth and shiny—about 20 to
30 minutes.

2. With gloves on, open the oven door and score the plastic into the
sizes you want, not smaller than ¾ by 1½ inch rectangles. Draw parallel
lines the length of the plastic mass and then draw parallel lines at right
angles to them. Refer back to Figure 5–2 if you have not used this
technique before.

Fig. 8-4

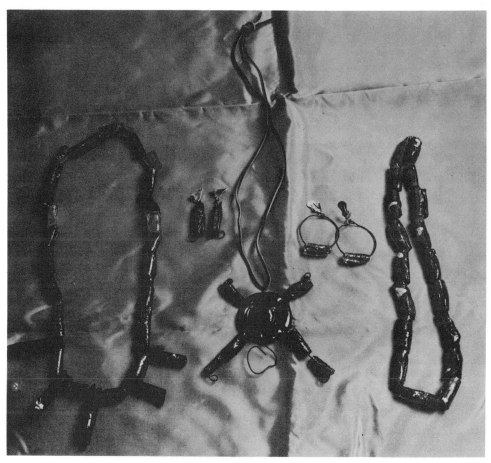

Jewelry made with mosaic beads. *From left:* pendant, drop earrings, medallion, loop earrings, and necklace.

Remove the cookie sheet from the oven and allow it to cool for about 20 minutes.

3. Lift the plastic from the foil and break it into rectangles along the scored lines. The pieces should snap apart.

4. Place 1 rectangle at a time, on a small piece of foil on the cookie sheet, into the oven. Heat for about 5 minutes.

Wearing the gloves, remove the cookie sheet from the oven. Wrap the plastic piece with the foil still on the back around the knitting needle as shown in Figure 8–5. Use the foil to help you roll the plastic around the needle. Peel away the foil. Make sure the bead is shaped as you want it: pinch the ends, but slip the bead off the needle so that the ends do not close.

Repeat step 4 until all the pieces of plastic have been turned into beads.

Fig. 8–5

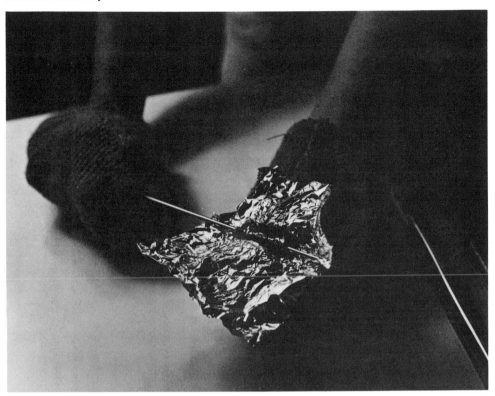

Hot mosaic piece is rolled over a metal knitting needle.

DROP EARRINGS

The wire will show on your finished earrings, so select wire that matches your findings—copper, gold, or silver color.

MATERIALS	EQUIPMENT
2, 4, or 6 beads, depending on their length	pliers
18 gauge wire, 6″ length	
1 pair drop earring findings	

1. Cut the wire into 2 lengths, 3 inches each. Using the pliers, turn a small loop in each wire but don't close the loops tightly. Thread the end of each loop through the circle at the base of each finding as shown in Figure 8–6. Use the pliers to close the loops, thereby attaching the wires permanently to the findings.

2. Thread the beads onto the dangling wires. Then use the pliers to turn up excess wire into a circular loop. The loop should be as neat as you can make it, but larger than the diameter of the bead's hole. This wire loop is decorative at the same time that it keeps the beads in place.

Fig. 8–6

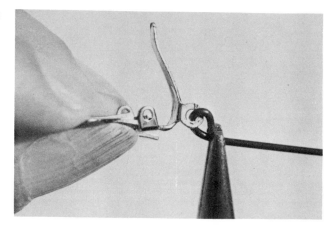

Turning the wire loop onto
your earring finding.

Fig. 8–7

Using a glass as a template to
form wire loops.

LOOP EARRINGS

Again, be sure to select wire in a color that matches your earring
findings.

MATERIALS	EQUIPMENT
2 beads	pliers
18 gauge wire, 8″ to 12″ long	2-ounce glass
1 pair drop earring findings	

1. Cut the wire into 2 lengths, either 4 or 6 inches long, depending on the size of the loop you want. Use a 2-ounce glass (shot glass) to turn each wire into an open circle (Fig. 8–7).

2. String a bead onto each wire, then twist the ends of each wire to close the circles. Form a loop out of the twisted ends and affix them to the loops on the findings, using pliers to close the wires tightly into the loops on the findings (see Fig. 8–4).

NECKLACE

This necklace can be as long or as short as you want it; try a choker or a 4-foot rope necklace.

MATERIALS	EQUIPMENT
20 to 40 beads, or more	pliers
jewelry wire or chain	
clasp (optional)	

1. Cut the wire or chain to the length you desire, and string the beads onto it.

2. Attach the clasp if it is necessary or desired (see step 4 under Pendant, earlier in this chapter). If the necklace is long enough to go over your head, you can knot the wire (making sure the raw ends are tucked in tightly) or link the ends of the chain together.

BEADED PENDANT

This pendant is shown at left in Figure 8–4.

MATERIALS	EQUIPMENT
29 beads	pliers
jewelry wire or chain	skewer
clasp (optional)	hot mitts

1. Heat the skewer and pierce 2 holes opposite each other at the top end of only 5 beads as shown in Figure 8–8.

2. String 10 beads onto the wire or chain. Then place the first "hanging" bead on the chain by inserting the wire or chain through the holes you just pierced in the top. Then alternate 1 regular bead with 1 hanging bead until all hanging beads are attached. Continue to string the remaining 10 beads.

3. Close the pendant, using a clasp, linking the ends of the chain together, or twisting the wires tightly so there are no raw ends to scratch you.

Fig. 8–8

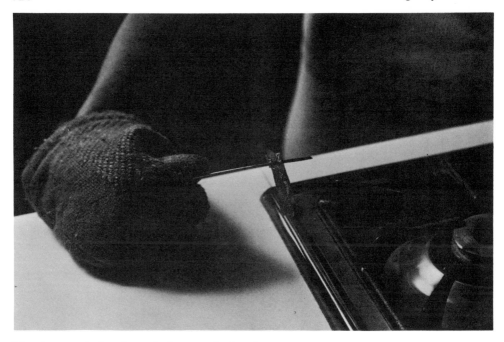

Piercing two holes through the top of a bead.

MEDALLION

The stunning medallion shown in Figure 8–4 (center) is slightly more complicated than the other jewelry, but well worth the effort!

MATERIALS	EQUIPMENT
2 round mosaic pieces, 1″ and 2″ in diameter	pliers
	aluminum foil
8 beads, ¾″ to 1″ long	cake pan
24″ of 18 gauge wire	2-ounce glass
chain or leather thong	

1. Cover the pan with a single layer of foil and lay the 2-inch round mosaic in the center of the pan.

2. Cut the wire into 3 equal lengths of 8 inches each. Place 1 wire on the 2-inch mosaic so that only 1 inch of the wire extends above the circle. The wire should also divide the circle in half.

Cross the other 2 wires at the center of the circle so that all 4 ends extend evenly as shown in Figure 8–9.

Place the 1-inch round mosaic over the wires at the center of the 2-inch mosaic (see Fig. 8–9). The wires will be fused between the 2 mosaics.

3. Place the pan into a 350° oven for 15 minutes. Use both ends of the 2-ounce glass (shot glass) to fuse and hammer the 2 plastic pieces.

Fig. 8–9

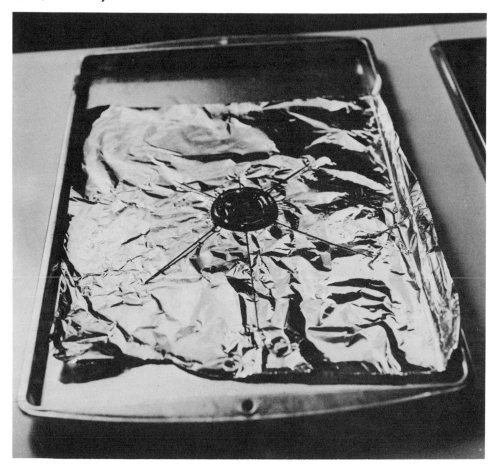

Wires are fused between two mosaic discs.

Allow the piece to cool for 20 minutes before lifting it off the foil.

4. String 2 beads onto each of the 4 crossed extending wires. Use the pliers to turn loops in the wire ends.

Form a curlicue of the 4-inch length of wire extending at the bottom of the medallion. To complete the necklace, form a loop in the top wire and insert the chain or thong through it.

CHAPTER 9

Realistic and Imaginary Flowers

YOU have probably already made two-dimensional realistic or imaginary flowers. There are endless combinations of colors, shapes, and sizes; you can alter the number and arrangement of petals; and you can add or omit pistils, stamens, and leaves at will. In this chapter, I'll give instructions for bending, shaping, and combining individual flower parts to create beautiful three-dimensional facsimiles; but first, I will discuss various handmade or bought leaves, then making two-dimensional flowers.

Considering all the possibilities, there can be no "wrong" flowers. Because of the transparent and brilliant nature of the crystals, anything you make is not only "right," but is very likely to be beautiful. Primitive or sophisticated, fragile and delicate or bold geometric "mod" flowers—all are gorgeous in their own right. It's up to you to decide which type blends best with the furnishings in the room you want to decorate with your "permanent flowers."

ALL MANNER OF LEAVES

How many and what kind of leaves you add to your plastic flowers is strictly a matter of choice. I will list several possibilities here; then, as you make your flower arrangements, decide which type is best for your flowers.

Cooking Crystal Leaves. If you wish to make your own, draw each leaf individually on aluminum foil and fill in the outline with green crystals. A wire, extending 2 to 3 inches beyond the leaf, should be embedded in the crystals before baking: you'll use the excess to attach it to the stem. You may want to shape the leaf immediately upon removal from the oven, or it can be used flat.

122

Embedded Craft Leaves. Craft and hobby stores sell packages of individual leaves made of cloth, plastic, or flocked paper. These leaves may be individually sandwiched between layers of green or transparent crystals. Although they usually come with stems attached, the stems are *not* heavy enough to bear the weight of the embedded leaf. Therefore, you should attach your own wire, embedding it in the crystals prior to baking. You may, of course, wish to use craft leaves without embedding them at all.

Real or Dried Leaves. If you remove the moisture from real leaves with the help of sodium silicate, you can embed these leaves in a sandwich of plastic granules. It is also possible to buy bunches of dried leaves from floral supply houses. These leaves can be removed from their branches and individually embedded.

Tissue Paper Leaves. Draw or color your own leaves on green tissue paper and embed them between two layers of green or transparent crystal, adding stem wire before baking.

Crepe Paper Leaves. Art supply houses have a wide spectrum of greens from which you can choose. Buy several shades and make big paper leaves just as you would for crepe paper Mexican flowers. Wrap stem wire around the bottom of the leaf, cover it with floral tape, and attach it to the

Fig. 9-1

Colorful plastic flowers can be "planted" in a pot.

stem of the plastic flower. Crepe paper leaves can also be individually embedded in plastic granules, using the same technique as tissue paper.

Artificial Leaves. You can buy small bunches of dried or artificial leaves and flowers already set up in attractive arrangements. These are quite striking when added as filler to your arrangement of plastic flowers.

Bunches of Live Leaves. If you are making a centerpiece or decoration for a specific event, arrange your plastic flowers in a basket or vase containing branches of leaves cut from a tree or bush. Although the leaves last for only a day or two, they make the most attractive bouquets.

Two-Dimensional Flowers

These plants fall into the category of imaginary flowers, although you can, of course, design them to look rather realistic. One of mine is shown in the color section, Figure 14, and another in Figure 9–1. Patterns for these are given in Figures 9–2 and 9–3, if you wish to use them; however, this is a good opportunity to design your own project.

I will discuss methods of making a flower in a solid piece with a plastic stem, and using a wire stem with the flower blossom made of cooking crystals, in the following projects.

FLOWERS WITH COOKING CRYSTAL STEMS

These can be "planted" right into a pot and make terrific windowsill decorations or party favors.

MATERIALS	EQUIPMENT
small amounts of cooking crystals in "flower colors"	cookie sheet
	aluminum foil
a larger amount of green crystals	felt tip pen or ball point pen
clay or plastic flower pot	spoon
green aquarium stones	hot mitts
	tweezers and brush
	tape (masking or cellophane)

1. Cover the cookie sheet with a length of aluminum foil, shiny side up. With the felt tip pen, draw a simple outline shape of a flower or trace a pattern from Figures 9–2 or 9–3 onto the foil. Make sure its size is appropriate to the flower pot. Take care that none of the flower parts are so delicate that they might be broken off from the body of the flower.

The stem must be 2 inches taller than the height of the pot and at least an inch wide to support the weight of the flower. Any leaves attached to the stem (optional) must be attached within the 2 inches closest to the head of the flower. If you wish to add stamens to the flower (see Fig. 9–1), lay them in place on the foil before spooning on the crystals.

Pattern for the flower shown in
the color section, Figure 14.

Fig. 9–2

Pattern for the flower in
Fig. 9–1.

Fig. 9–3

2. Spoon the crystals ⅛- to ¼-inch deep onto the foil drawing. Place adjoining colors next to each other with no spaces between them. Pick out any stray granules that fall into the wrong color with the tweezers. Push the granules along the outside edges of the flower into a smooth line with the side of your finger or a brush.

3. Place the cookie sheet into the oven at 350° for approximately 30 minutes or until the crystals fuse into a smooth, shiny mass.

Remove the cookie sheet from the oven and allow the flower to cool for about 20 minutes. Then lift it away from the aluminum foil.

4. Put a strip of tape over the hole on the inside bottom of the pot or place a circle of cardboard in it to prevent the stones from falling out.

Place the bottom of the stem down in the center of the pot. Hold the flower upright with one hand while you pour the stones around the stem. Continue pouring the stones until their weight supports the flower in its upright position—usually within an inch of the top of the pot.

CRYSTAL BLOSSOMS WITH WIRE STEMS

If you use heavy stem wire or even coat hanger wire instead of the thick strip of plastic for stems to support the flower heads, the flowers look more delicate. You can therefore arrange 2 or 3 flowers in a single pot or vase more attractively.

MATERIALS	EQUIPMENT
cooking crystals in "flower colors"	cookie sheet
clay or plastic flower pot	aluminum foil
green aquarium stones	felt tip pen
14, 16, or 18 gauge wire (or	spoon
straightened coat hanger wire	hot mitts
green floral tape	tweezers and brush
	tape
	wire cutters
	pliers
	ruler

1. Cover the cookie sheet with a single piece of aluminum foil, shiny side up. With the felt tip pen, draw a simple outline of the flower head only near one end of the cookie sheet.

2. Cut a length of stem wire that equals the diameter of the flower head plus the height of the flower pot plus 2 inches. The wire must not be longer than the cookie sheet, however, as the wire must lie flat during the baking process so that it is held firmly in the molten crystals.

3. From the top to the bottom of the flower head, spoon a strip of cooking crystals measuring about a half inch across and about ⅛-inch deep. Lay the stem wire on top of the strip of crystals. Then spoon more crystals onto the foil, filling in your flower outline. Essentially, you have made a sandwich of the wire between the two layers of crystal (Fig. 9–4).

Fig. 9–4

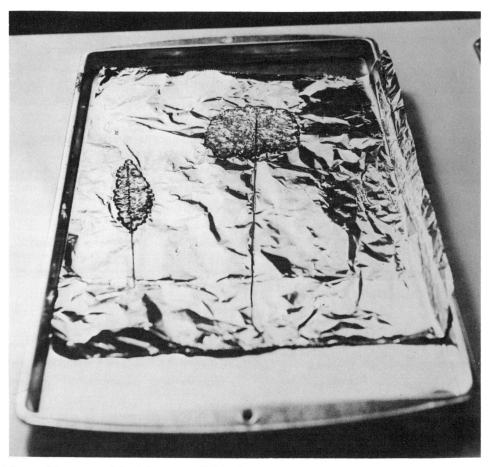

Flower blossom and leaf drawn on foil with wire stems sandwiched between layers of crystals.

The wire will be slightly visible in the blossom after it has been baked, but it will not really detract from its beauty and you will have a secure bond between the flower and its stem.

4. If you wish, you can draw leaves on the same piece of foil. The leaves should not be attached to the flower or to each other; just draw them in corners where they will not interfere with the design.

Spoon a thin layer of green crystals down the center of the leaf. Cut a length of wire the same length as the leaf plus at least 2 inches. Lay the wire on the bed of crystals with the extra 2 inches extending at the base of the leaf. Cover the entire leaf with additional green crystals to a depth of ⅛ inch (see Fig. 9–4).

5. Place the cookie sheet into the oven at 350° for approximately 30 minutes or until the crystals are smooth and shiny.

Remove the cookie sheet from the oven and allow the flower parts to cool for approximately 20 minutes before lifting them off the foil.

Fig. 9–5

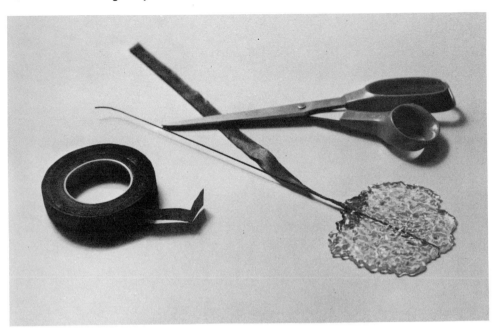

Wrapping floral tape around the stem diagonally.

6. To assemble the flower, first tear off a piece of floral tape approximately 12 inches long. Although the tape doesn't seem sticky, it does adhere to itself. Start wrapping it around the stem wire at the base of the flower (Fig. 9–5). Overlap the tape as you work downwards.

If you are adding leaves, remember to attach them within 2 inches of the flower head. First, bend the wire at the base of the leaf to a 45° angle with your pliers (Fig. 9–6). Then, as you wrap the tape on the main stem, you can just include the leaf stem within the wrapping.

When you have used up the 12-inch piece of tape, simply tear off another piece and continue wrapping where you left off until the entire stem is covered (Fig. 9–7).

If you are making 2 or 3 flowers to put in one pot, vary the lengths of the stem wires so that the flowers will not all be the same height. This makes for a prettier, more flexible arrangement (Fig. 9–8).

7. Tape or cover the hole at the bottom of the flower pot from the inside. Pour the colored stones into the pot until it is half full. Center the stem of the tallest flower and push it down through the stones. Position the stems of other flowers and push them down into the stones. Add additional stones up to the top of the pot so that the flowers are held in place.

Using Molds to Make Three-Dimensional Flowers

Three-dimensional flowers can be either realistic or imaginary, but working in a third dimension seems to promote the idea of creating

Fig. 9-6

Leaves are attached by wrapping them right along with the stem.

Fig. 9-7

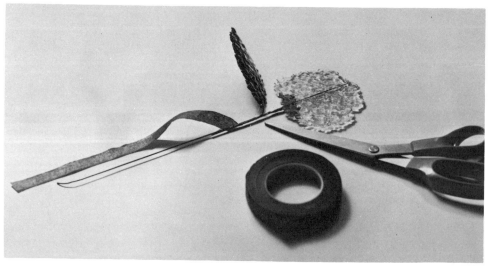

Stem is completely covered with floral tape.

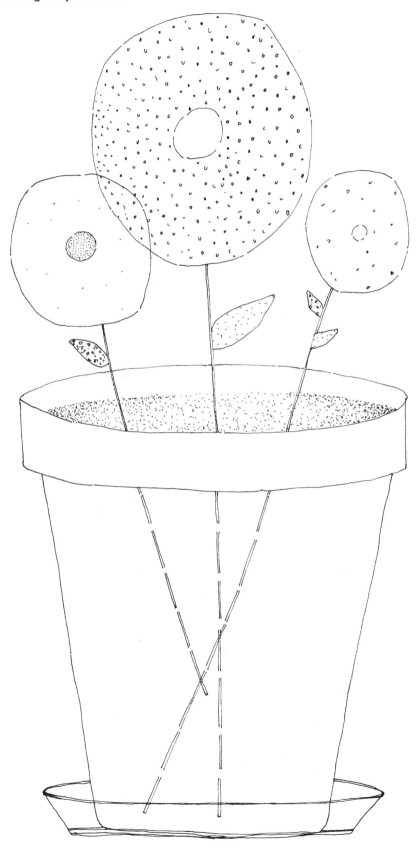

Heights of flowers are varied in this arrangement.

likenesses. Therefore, the floral arrangements I am including here are made up of "realistic" flowers.

In this section I'll discuss three methods of making three-dimensional flowers in kitchen molds, then include some suggestions for other methods you might try. The following section will deal with shaping flowers by hand from prebaked plastic shapes. Both techniques require the manipulation of the warm plastic as it comes from the oven—and speed! If you can picture yourself in cotton gloves and track shoes, you're ready to begin.

In describing these methods, I will give directions for making one flower at a time; however, you can make several in one baking by filling the molds simultaneously. Place them all on a cookie sheet for baking, remove them from the molds when cool, and return them to the oven one at a time just prior to manipulation and assembly.

USING MOLDS: METHOD I

Metal tart molds, as I mentioned in Chapter 3, come in a wide variety of shapes, flutings, and sizes. Some even look like daisies or posies, and all of them make perfect flower blossoms.

MATERIALS	EQUIPMENT
cooking crystals	metal tart mold(s)
18 gauge stem wire	spoon
floral tape	tweezers
bowl, basket, or short vase	pliers
florist's clay	wire cutter
bouquet of leaves, fresh or artificial	hot mitts
transparent epoxy	cotton gloves
plastic stamens and	cookie sheet
calyx (optional)	aluminum foil

1. Place a thin layer of crystals on the bottom of the mold. The depth can be ⅛ inch or less. With your fingers, push the crystals up the sides of the mold as far as they will go without falling back.

If you'd like to have a different colored center, clear a circle in the middle of the crystals with your finger. Spoon the second (or even a third) color into the well you have made (Fig. 9–9). The different colors of crystal should be touching, but not overlapping. If stray granules fall outside their color area, remove them with the tweezers.

You can also set glass or plastic jewels in the center. The surrounding crystals will keep the jewels permanently in place.

2. Set the mold into a 350° oven for approximately 20 minutes. The size of the mold and the depth of the crystals will affect the baking time.

Fig. 9–9

Spooning in a different color for the flower's center.

Remove the mold from the oven when the plastic is soft and shiny. Since you cannot remove the crystal from the mold until it has cooled, you must wait about 15 minutes. Do not place the mold in the refrigerator or in cold water: this will not harm the plastic and will even speed up the cooling process, but the fast change in temperature will warp your mold and may make it impossible to use again.

3. Place the unmolded flower head on a foil-covered cookie sheet. Return it to the 350° oven for about 5 minutes—just long enough to make the plastic pliable.

Wearing cotton gloves, remove the flower head from the oven and quickly bend, twist, or ruffle the outer edges into a shape pleasing to you. Hold the flower in this position until it cools (only a matter of seconds).

4. Cut a length of stem wire appropriate to the size of the flower head and to the size of the bowl or vase you are using.

I'll describe 3 methods of attaching the wire to the flower head. Read them through and decide which method you'd like to try.

A. Hold the end of the wire in an open flame. Pierce the center of the flower blossom from back to front with the hot wire. Use the pliers to turn the wire end into a small tight loop, just big enough to prevent the wire from slipping back through the hole (Fig. 9–10). If you are

Fig. 9–10

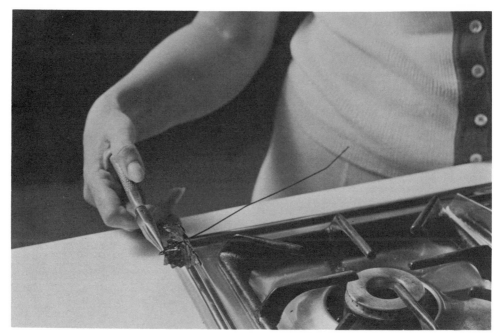

The center of the molded flower is pierced with a heated wire before the wire is turned into a loop.

Fig. 9–11

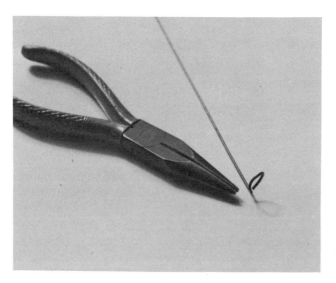

The end of the wire is bent into a loop, then angled.

deft with the pliers and can turn a very small loop, this method provides the most durable bond. If you are unable to make the loop small enough, however, the wire loop on the face of the flower may prove to be unattractive.

B. With the pliers, bend the last inch of the wire into a loop or spiral. Use the pliers again to bend the loop or spiral at a right angle to the rest of the stem as shown in Figure 9–11. Hold the loop over an

Fig. 9–12

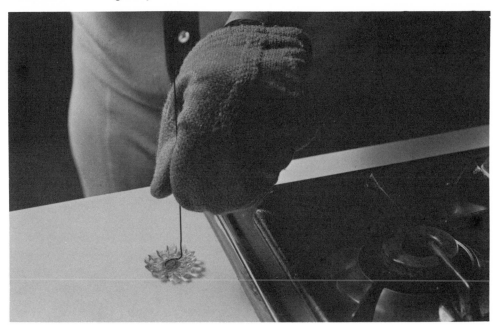

The wire loop is heated and fused—or simply glued—onto back of flower.

open flame until the wire is red hot. Then quickly press it into the back of the flower head so that it makes a depression in the plastic at the same time it fuses to it (Fig. 9–12).

C. Make the same type of loop and bend it as in **B**, but glue the loop to the back of the flower head with transparent epoxy instead of heating and fusing it.

5. Tear off a 12-inch length of floral tape. Beginning at the top, wrap the tape around the stem wire. Overlap the tape as you go. Tear off additional lengths of tape as you need them.

6. Plastic stamens and calyx are not necessary additions, but they add a more realistic touch. The calyx is the green cap at the top of the stem from which the flower head emerges. Just slide one up the stem from the bottom and glue it into place (Fig. 9–13). The stamens are merely decorative; they add color to the center of the flower. They are inserted by heating a wire wrapped around a small bunch of them. Most hobby stores sell these floral accents (Fig. 9–14). If you cannot find them locally, see the Source of Supply listing.

7. To assemble the arrangement, place florist's clay at the bottom of the bowl, vase, or basket and insert the flower stems into the clay. Add as many flowers as you wish, varying the heights of their stems. Place them into the arrangement at attractive angles. Complete the arrangement by filling in the empty spaces with bunches of real or artificial leaves. Cover the floral clay with colored stones only if it is visible and unattractive.

Fig. 9-13

Sliding a plastic calyx up over the stem before wrapping.

USING MOLDS: METHOD II

In this technique, you'll use a 2-stage procedure; remember that you can easily make 6 or 8 flowers at one time.

MATERIALS	EQUIPMENT
cooking crystals	a round tart mold
18 gauge stem wire	a smaller fluted metal mold
floral tape	spoon
bowl, basket, or short vase	tweezers
florist's clay	pliers
bouquet of fresh or plastic leaves	wire cutter
	cotton gloves
	hot mitts
	baking sheet

1. Spoon crystals into the bottom of the round tart mold. Make the layer of crystals thin—no more than ⅛-inch high. Arrange the crystals in any design, combination of colors, or in concentric circles.

2. Place the mold into a 350° oven for approximately 15 minutes or until the plastic is smooth and shiny.

Remove the mold from the oven and allow it to cool about 10 minutes or until you can easily remove the plastic disc from the mold.

3. Invert the fluted mold on top of a baking sheet for ease in handling. Center the plastic disc (which must be larger in diameter than the base of the mold) over the bottom of the fluted mold as shown in Figure 9–15.

Fig. 9–14

Floral accents: Crystal Cast, stamens, cloth leaves, floral wire, calyx, and floral tape. *(Crystal Cast® manufactured by Joli Plastics Corp.).*

Fig. 9–15

The disc is shaped by heating it over an inverted tart mold.

Place the baking sheet with the mold and plastic disc on it into the oven. As the plastic is reheated, the disc will drape and fold down over the sides of the mold. Watch the process carefully, as it happens very quickly and you will want to remove the flower head from the oven at just the right time. Wearing cotton gloves, you can still alter the shape of the flower, but generally the natural contours are most attractive.

4. Attach the flower head to the stem, using one of the techniques described in method I, step 4. The stem may be attached within the cup or on the back of the cup; it depends only on your concept of the flower you are making.

Wrap the stem, including leaves, then add a calyx or stamen if you wish, as in steps 5 and 6, method I.

Assemble the arrangement as described in method I or according to your own ideas. There is no reason that you cannot combine flowers made with various methods into a single arrangement (Fig. 9–16).

USING MOLDS: METHOD III

This time, you're going to make separate petals and then combine them into a single flower.

MATERIALS	EQUIPMENT
cooking crystals in 2 colors	5 candy molds, same design
18 gauge stem wire	spoon
floral tape	cotton gloves
bowl, basket, or short vase	hot mitts
florist's clay	baking sheet
bouquet of fresh or artificial leaves	aluminum foil
floral accents (optional)	wire cutters
	pliers

1. If you have 5 molds of the same size and design, fill them all with the same color crystals and place them in a 350° oven only until the crystals in each mold have fused. You do not have to leave them in the oven until they are smooth, as this method requires a second baking. As soon as they have cooled enough to handle, remove the plastic petals from the molds.

If you have only 1 mold, reuse it so that you have a total of 5 petals. You can, of course, modify this method to make as many petals per flower as you like.

2. Place a length of aluminum foil over the surface of the baking sheet. In the center of it, place a teaspoon full of crystals, in a color complementary to the petals. Then arrange the 5 petals around the cooking crystal center so that they are touching one another and overlapping the center as shown in Figure 9–17.

3. Return the flower to the 350° oven and bake until the petals are smooth and glossy and all parts are fused.

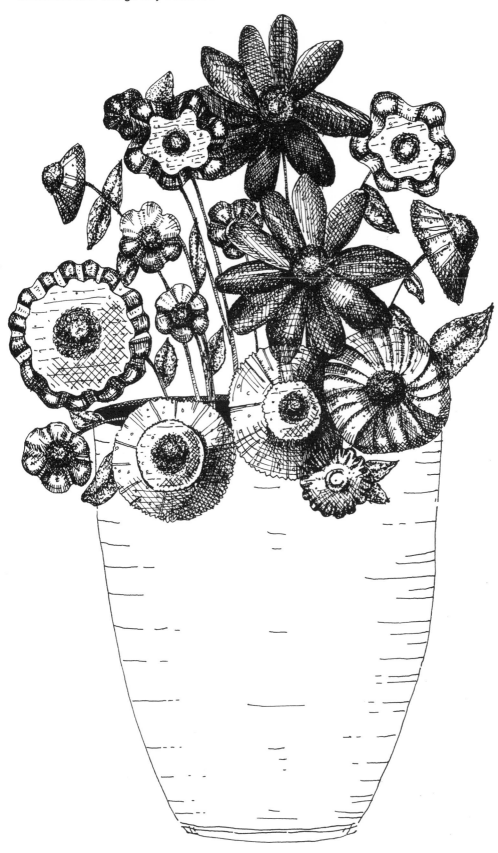

Combining flowers made with various methods into one arrangement.

Fig. 9–17

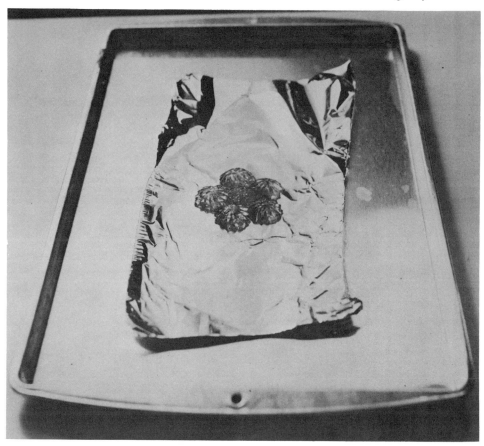

Five petals arranged around a crystal center.

Wearing the cotton gloves, remove the flower from the oven and gently bend the petals as you wish. Hold them in position for several seconds until the plastic hardens.

Complete the flowers and assemble the arrangement as described in steps 4 through 7, method I.

USING MOLDS: POTPOURRI OF METHODS

Without presenting detailed projects, I would like to mention several alternative possibilities for making flowers in molds. With some imagination, you might combine various methods with these, or dream up your very own techniques.

Unbaked Flowers or Accents. You can mold cooking crystals *without the use of heat* with Crystal Cast®, a liquid solvent. When Crystal Cast is poured over the unbaked crystals, they become tacky and stick to each other like popcorn covered with molasses.

If you pour the liquid over a tablespoon of green crystals, you can form a calyx directly around the stem of a flower by hand. The crystals are flexible at first—you can mold petals or an entire blossom—but it will dry in the air at room temperature in a couple of hours and become completely rigid. Any project you make with unbaked crystals and Crystal Cast will look exactly like what it is—unbaked crystals stuck together!

Cookie Cutter Flowers. Although the technique varies slightly, you can adapt cookie cutters to the procedures in methods I, II, and III. If you are using the style of cookie cutter that is open at the top and bottom, place it on aluminum foil on a cookie sheet. Spoon crystals into the cutter to a depth of ⅛ inch or less. (Remember that the solder used in making cookie cutters of this type does not always withstand oven temperature; the cutter may not be reusable unless you resolder the joint.) Place the cookie sheet into a 350° oven for about 20 minutes or until the crystals look smooth and shiny. Remove the cookie sheet from the oven and allow the piece to cool for 20 minutes before pushing it out of the cookie cutter shape.

If you're using cookie cutters with built-in handles, the method differs. Spread an even layer of crystals directly on a foil-covered cookie sheet over an area slightly larger than the cookie cutter you are planning to use. Place the crystals in the 350° oven until the plastic is smooth and shiny. Open the oven door, and with a hot mitt on your hand, press the cookie cutter firmly into the plastic. Immediately remove the cookie sheet from the oven and allow everything to cool. After 20 minutes, lift off the cookie cutter. If any of the excess pieces are still attached to the plastic shape, you can easily snap them off.

Once you have made your plastic shapes with either method, the flowers can be finished according to the directions in methods I, II, or III above.

Making Three-Dimensional Flowers without Molds

When using this method, you mentally dissect a real flower in order to duplicate its parts in plastic. The shape of the petals forms your basic pattern. The plastic parts are baked and, while still warm and pliable, are molded and fused to one another to recreate the whole.

I'll describe in detail the construction of three flowers shown in color Figure 15: a rose, a tulip, and a carnation. When you become familiar with the processes involved, you can go on to create a facsimile of nearly any flower you wish. Just study the component parts of the flower and with a "pattern" in mind, recombine the processes to evoke the effect you want. Work fast and wear gloves!

ROYAL ROSE

A perfect rose is so beautiful you might want to make a dozen American Beauties as a very special gift.

Fig. 9–18

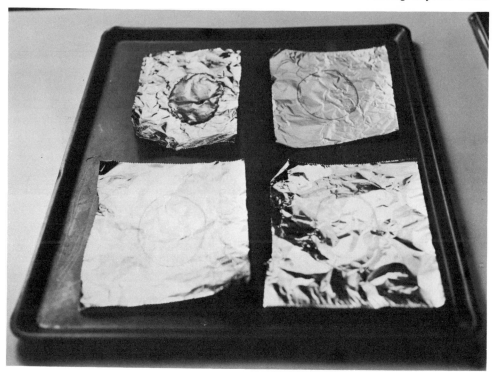

Four rose petals are baked at one time.

MATERIALS	EQUIPMENT
8 ounces cooking crystals	cookie sheet
18, 16, or 14 gauge stem wire	aluminum foil
floral tape	scissors
	felt tip pen
	cotton gloves
	spoon
	wire cutter
	pliers
	brush

1. Cut 8 pieces of aluminum foil, each measuring 4 by 6 inches. Smooth out the foil and lay the pieces flat on top of the cookie sheet. If they don't all fit, save the extras for a second shift.

With a felt tip pen, draw an oval shape measuring approximately 2 inches wide by 3½ inches long on each foil rectangle.

2. Spoon a single layer of the same color crystal into each of the oval shapes (Fig. 9–18). Smooth the outer edges by gently pushing against the crystals with the side of your index finger or a brush. Place the cookie sheet into a 350° oven for approximately 15 minutes—or until all the ovals are smooth and glossy.

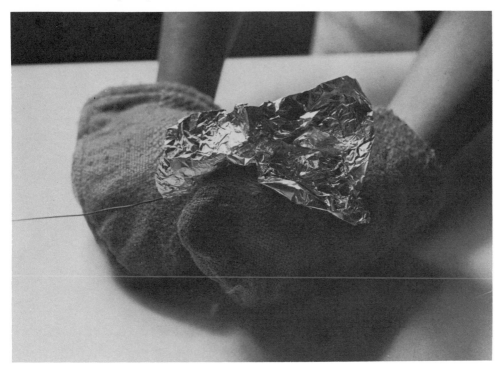

Wrap one petal around the stem wire.

3. Meanwhile, cut a length of stem wire approximately 12 inches long. Using the pliers, bend a half-inch loop at one end of the wire. Then bend the loop at a 45° angle to the stem.

4. When the crystals have finished baking, remove the cookie sheet from the oven and *immediately* wrap one oval lengthwise around the looped end of the stem wire (Fig. 9–19). Use the foil to help you wrap; then peel it off the petal. This first oval is the center petal of the rose: the bottom should be wrapped around the loop as tightly as possible to keep the stem permanently attached and the top of it should be slightly flared. If it hardens before you have arranged it just so, return it with the wire to the oven for a few minutes and then rework it.

5. Return a single oval to the oven on its foil rectangle for about 3 minutes or until the plastic is pliable. (Since you will be working with just one petal at a time, return them individually to the oven for reheating as you need them.)

Remove the second oval from the oven and press it around the outside of the first oval about ¼-inch up from the base so that the top of the new oval is slightly higher. While you are pressing and squeezing the base of this petal with one hand in order to fuse it to the center by means of its heat, you are turning out the top of the petal to give it shape with your other hand. Peel away the foil after the petal is shaped and in place.

Note: Each succeeding petal should adhere or fuse to the others as its heat softens the surrounding plastic. This theory does not always work in practice, however, so it doesn't hurt to have some transparent epoxy handy—just in case.

6. Reheat the next petal. Add it to the flower by overlapping the second petal at the base about a quarter to a half inch higher. Flare the top outwards.

7. Add the fourth petal in the same manner: the center plus the first 3 petals form a bud. Continue adding petals around it, overlapping the petals at the base and flaring them more widely at the top to form a full and well-shaped rose.

Attach a calyx if you want one, then cover the stem with floral tape, adding leaves as you wrap.

A TULIP

Add a touch of spring to your home all year round with a colorful tulip.

MATERIALS	EQUIPMENT
cooking crystals	cookie sheet
18, 16, or 14 gauge stem wire	aluminum foil
floral tape	felt tip pen
	ruler
	cotton gloves
	spoon
	hot mitts
	wire cutter
	pliers
	brush

1. Place a 10 x 12 inch piece of aluminum foil on the cookie sheet. Using the felt tip pen, draw a circle 7 inches in diameter on the foil. At the center of the circle, draw another circle 1 inch in diameter. Radiating outwards from this center circle to the circumference of the 7-inch circle, draw a flower shape consisting of 5 petals (Fig. 9–20). Each petal should be about 2½ to 3 inches long, 2 inches wide, and well separated from the petals on either side of it.

2. Spoon crystals into the petal shapes and the center circle to a height of $1/16$ to $1/8$ of an inch. Smooth the outer edges of the petals by pushing gently against the granules with the side of your index finger or a brush.

3. Cut a length of stem wire approximately 15 inches long. Turn the wire down with the pliers 3 inches from one end to form a U turn. Then twist this end of the wire around the stem to form a narrow oval about 2 inches long and ¼- to ½-inch wide. Lay the wire on a separate piece of

Fig. 12
Combine your own imagination with cooking crystals to produce bowls and dishes as elegant as these.

Fig. 13
Tissue paper drawings can be sandwiched between layers of crystals for any effect you want—including this charming "happy face."

Fig. 14
Two-dimensional flowers with plastic stems can be "planted" in a pot for a colorful window-sill decoration.

Fig. 15
Delicate three-dimensional flowers are individually shaped by hand, then combined for an exquisite—and permanent—floral arrangement.

Fig. 9-20

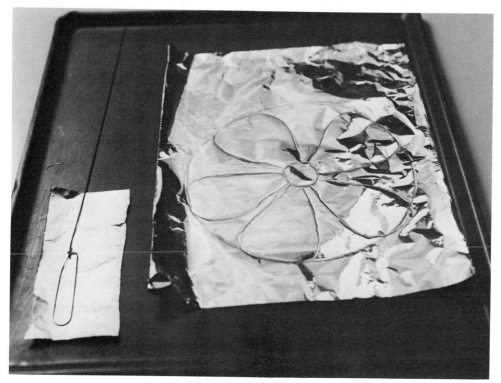

Tulip shape and wire pistil are filled with crystals.

aluminum foil on the cookie sheet so that the oval lies flat (see Fig. 9–20). Fill the oval with either green or black cooking crystals. This will be the tulip's pistil.

4. Place the cookie sheet into a 350° oven and bake until the parts are smooth and glossy—about 20 to 25 minutes.

5. Wearing gloves, remove the cookie sheet from the oven. Immediately turn the 5 petals down into a cup shape by turning 2 opposite petals down first and then overlapping the 3 remaining petals (Fig. 9–21). Let the aluminum foil help you, but don't let it get trapped between the plastic petals. If the piece hardens before you get the shape you want, place the flower over an inverted glass and return it to the oven for a few minutes; you can then complete the shaping with the help of gravity. Peel away the foil.

6. Hold the plain end of the stem wire in an open flame until the wire is red hot. From the *inside of the tulip*, push the hot wire down and through the crystals so that the stem comes out at the bottom center of the tulip and the pistil rests on the inside.

7. Wrap floral tape tightly around the stem to prevent the flower from slipping down and continue wrapping the stem, adding leaves as desired.

Fig. 9–21

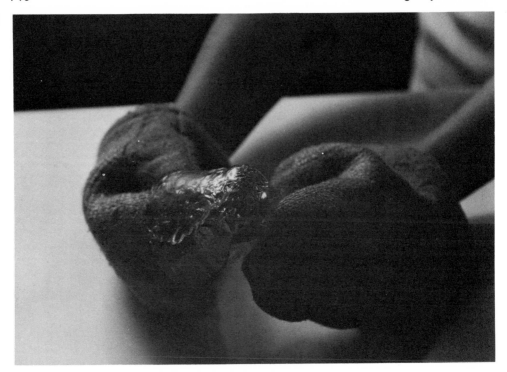

Turn petals down into tulip shape while plastic is hot.

A CARNATION

Modify the stem length for a permanent boutonniere.

MATERIALS	EQUIPMENT
cooking crystals	cookie sheet
18, 16, or 14 gauge wire	aluminum foil
floral tape	felt tip pen
	ruler
	scissors
	spoon
	wire cutter
	cotton gloves

1. Cut 3 squares of aluminum foil, each 6 by 6 inches, and place on the cookie sheet. With a felt tip pen, draw a 2-inch circle in the center of one square, a 3¼-inch circle on the second square, and a 4½-inch circle on the third square.

2. Spoon the same color crystals on all 3 circles to a depth of ⅛ inch. Using the tip of your index finger, push the crystals in around the circles' circumferences to create scallops ⅛- to ¼-inch deep (Fig. 9–22).

3. Place the cookie sheet in the oven at 350° and bake until the plastic looks smooth and shiny.

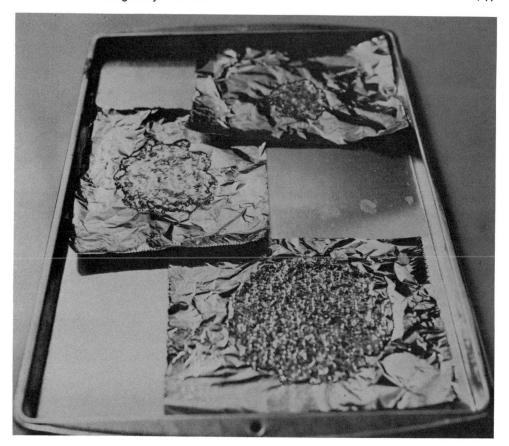

Three circles are needed to form a carnation.

4. Wearing your work gloves, remove the 2-inch circle from the oven. Press down in the center of the circle with the thumb of one hand while you cup the circle upwards with your other hand (Fig. 9–23). Quickly pinch the bottom of the circle on the outside while you flute the scalloped edges and turn them slightly outward; then peel off the foil. If the piece becomes too rigid to work with, return it to the oven briefly and continue when the plastic softens.

5. Open the oven door and immediately press the formed 2-inch circle into the center of the 3¼-inch circle. Remove the cookie sheet from the oven, and quickly pick up and shape the 3¼-inch circle around the 2-inch circle, fluting the edges as you go (Fig. 9–24). Peel away the foil.

6. Return the 4½-inch circle to the oven on the cookie sheet to soften the plastic. When it looks ready, open the oven door and set the first 2 sections into the center of the circle as shown in Figure 9–25. Remove the cookie sheet from the oven.

Quickly pick up the 3 pieces, working the edges of the last circle *down* (not up, as you did the first 2), fluting the edges as you go. Peel away the foil.

Fig. 9-23

Forming and shaping the smallest circle.

Fig. 9-24

Forming the second circle around the smaller one.

7. Cut a length of stem wire about 10 to 12 inches long. Place one end of it over an open flame until the wire is red hot. Push the wire through the bottom center of the flower, piercing all 3 layers, but barely visible in the center of the flower. Hold the wire in place until the plastic solidifies around it.

For increased security, spread a little glue at the joint before you wrap the floral tape around the stem.

Fig. 9-25

The first two circles are set onto the third and its edges are turned down.

CHAPTER 10

Windchimes, Mobiles, and Hanging Lamps

⧉⧉ FANTASTIC windchimes and mobiles can be constructed from a number of discs or shapes made of cooking crystals and strung or wired together. The finished product is freely suspended and must be light weight enough so that its parts move when they are jostled about by slight air currents.

You'll want to string the discs of a windchime close enough to each other to produce the pleasant bell-like chimes as the breezes cause the discs to hit one against another. I have included instructions for two windchimes, or you might want to design your own.

A mobile's parts may or may not strike each other as they move about on the ends of their wires: it's up to you.

The charming hanging lamp is a special project included in this chapter because constructing and assembling it is very similar to making a windchime.

SINGING WINDCHIMES

The discs can be multicolored, with or without variation in design.

MATERIALS	EQUIPMENT
cooking crystals in several colors	a 12-cup muffin tin
nylon cord	cookie sheet
	aluminum foil
	felt tip pen
	ruler
	scissors
	spoon
	hot mitts
	skewer

Fig. 10-1

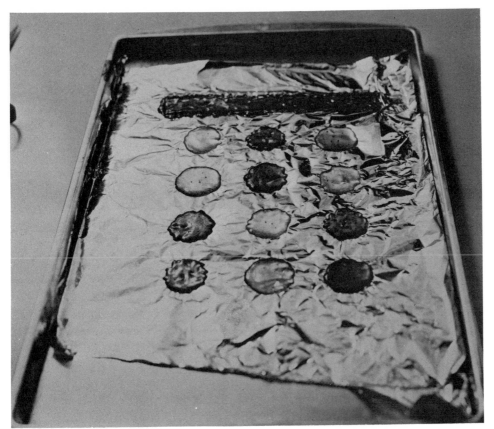

Draw a rectangle at one end of the foil, spaced well apart from the discs.

1. Spoon cooking crystals into each compartment of the muffin tin, making the layers of crystals no higher than $^1/_{16}$ of an inch. You can keep each disc a solid color, or mix 2 colors in each compartment.

2. Place the muffin tin into the oven at 350° until the crystal granules have fused but are still grainy.

Remove the muffin tin from the oven, allow it to cool for about 15 minutes, and turn the 12 discs out of the pan. If they do not fall out easily, rap the pan sharply against the side of the kitchen counter.

3. Cover the cookie sheet with a length of aluminum foil. Along one end, draw a rectangle measuring 8 inches by 1 inch. Make sure it is at least an inch away from the edge of the foil on all sides. Fill in the rectangle with cooking crystals to a depth of about ⅛ inch (Fig. 10–1).

4. Place the 12 discs upside down on the foil with as much space as possible between them (see Fig. 10–1). Return the cookie sheet to the oven until the rectangle looks smooth and shiny and the discs are very thin and flat. Remove the cookie sheet from the oven and allow all pieces to cool 15 to 20 minutes. Lift the pieces from the foil.

5. Wearing a hot mitt, heat and reheat the skewer in order to puncture holes at the *top and bottom of 9 of the discs,* and *only the top of 3 of the discs.*

Fig. 10-2

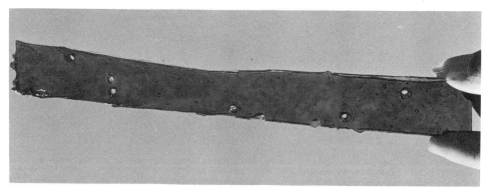

Pierce two holes at the top of the rectangle, with 3 holes along the bottom.

Fig. 10-3

Thread and knot the discs into three rows of four discs each.

Holding the rectangle horizontally, puncture a total of 5 holes as follows: 3 holes should be ¼ inch up from the bottom, 2 inches in from either end with one in the center; and 2 holes should be ¼ inch down from

Fig. 10–4

Each row of discs is securely attached to the cooking crystal rectangle.

the top and 1 inch in from either end. Hole positioning can be seen clearly in Figure 10–2.

6. Place the discs in 3 rows of 4 each. A disc having only *one* hole should be at the bottom of each row. To string the first row, cut a 2-foot length of cord, thread it through the bottom disc and tie a knot. Leave about an inch of free cord between discs and continue stringing through both holes of 3 more discs, tying knots in the cord to keep the discs in place (Fig. 10–3). Attach the end of the cord through one of the bottom holes of the rectangle. Tie a secure knot and cut off the excess cord.

String the other 2 rows of discs in the same manner and attach them to the rectangle as shown in Figure 10–4.

Fig. 10-5

Individual mosaics are framed with lead to make windchimes.

Cut another length of cord 12 to 15 inches long. Tie the ends through the 2 upper holes in the rectangle and use this cord to hang the windchimes from a nail or hook attached to the wall, ceiling, or on your front porch.

MOSAIC WINDCHIMES

Use any mosaic shapes and patterns you want; irregular outline shapes are most attractive (Fig. 10-5); although the sizes need not be identical, they should be roughly 3 by 3 inches.

MATERIALS	EQUIPMENT
a 12″ length of ½″ dowel	soldering iron
5 mosaics	spool of 60/40 solder
nylon cord	metal skewer
30″ U-shaped lead came	scissors
	hot mitts
	pliers
	glue (optional)

1. Stretch the lead came and measure and cut lengths to the circumference of the mosaics. With the help of the pliers, shape a lead strip around each mosaic piece, soldering the ends of the lead closed.

2. Heat the metal skewer and pierce a hole where you want the *top* of each mosaic piece to be.

Fig. 10–6

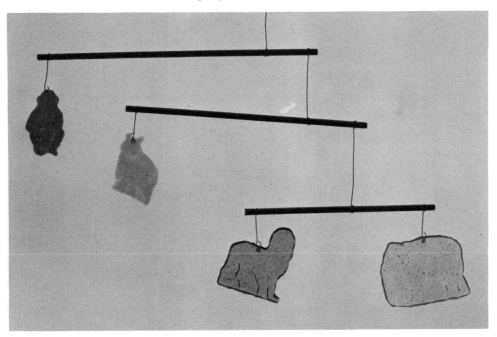

The finished jungle mobile.

3. Cut five 8-inch lengths of nylon cord. String one through the hole in each mosaic piece and knot securely. Tie the other end of the cord around the dowel so that the pieces are centered, evenly spaced, and overlap about a half inch. The windchime is more attractive, however, if you stagger the lengths of cord holding the mosaics (see Fig. 10–5).

4. Cut a length of cord 15 inches long and tie the ends to each end of the dowel. You may want to use glue to hold all of the knots securely in place. Hang the windchimes by centering the top cord over a nail or hook.

Note: If you do not have mosaic pieces, you can just shape strips of lead came into free-form designs and solder the ends. Then place the lead shapes on a foil-covered cookie sheet, fill them with cooking crystals, and bake them until the crystal is smooth and shiny. After the shapes have cooled, follow steps 2 through 5. You may also paint a strip of lightweight wood and punch holes in it to substitute for the dowel.

JUNGLE MOBILE

I arbitrarily chose the lion, elephant, bear, and monkey from the 9 designs on an aluminum foil cookie mold for the jungle mobile shown in Figure 10–6. You may, of course, use any molds you choose, draw designs freehand on aluminum foil, or use completed lead shapes.

The instructions are for a mobile with 4 adornments and 3 rods, but you could add as many designs or additional rods as you wish.

Fig. 10-7

Filling the animal shapes in an aluminum foil tray.

MATERIALS	EQUIPMENT
cooking crystals in "animal colors"	foil animal cookie mold
½" dowel in 3 lengths: 8", 10", and 12"	spoon
	skewer
spool of jewelry wire	scissors
	table knife
	hot mitts
	glue

1. Spoon cooking crystals into the 4 designs you want to use (Fig. 10–7). Push stray granules back into place with your finger; smooth the surface the same way.

2. Place the mold into a 350° oven until the plastic looks smooth and shiny—about 20 minutes. Remove the mold from the oven and allow it to cool for another 10 to 15 minutes before releasing the designs.

3. Heat the skewer or ice pick in an open flame and pierce a hole through the top of each piece.

Use the table knife to lightly score both ends of all dowels about a half inch in from the ends.

4. Study Figure 10–6 closely as you complete steps 4 through 8—the photograph will help substantially with the assembly of the mobile.

Cut a piece of wire about 3 inches long. Twist and tie one end of it through the hole in the lion and the other end of it around the score mark on one end of the 8-inch dowel. If the wire slips about on the dowel and does not seem secure, use a dab of glue to keep it in place.

Cut another piece of wire about 3 inches long. Twist and tie one end of it through the hole in the top of the elephant, and fasten the other end of the wire over the remaining end of the 8-inch dowel.

5. Using 3-inch lengths of wire, attach the bear to one end of the 10-inch dowel and attach the monkey to one end of the 12-inch dowel.

6. Cut a 6-inch length of wire and pick up the dowel with the lion and the elephant attached to it. Find the balance point of the dowel (not necessarily the center) by holding it on the edge of the table knife and adjusting the dowel back and forth until it balances on the knife edge without falling off. Tie the piece of wire tightly around this point, using glue if necessary to hold it in place. Leave about 2 inches of wire exposed and fasten the free end of the wire at the score mark on the 10-inch dowel. Cut off any excess wire.

7. Using the table knife again, find the balance point of the 10-inch dowel and tie and glue a 6-inch piece of wire at that point. Leave 2 inches of wire exposed, and tie the free end of the wire onto the 12-inch dowel at the score line.

8. Using the table knife, find the balance point of the 12-inch dowel. Tie a long piece of wire at that point so that you can hang your finished mobile from the ceiling or wherever it has room to move freely.

HANGING LAMP

The hanging lamp is a simple, but extremely attractive, matter of baking and stringing an incredible number of cooking crystal discs— 268 of them, to be exact. If you have the patience, and want the excitement of sending off to Denmark for the lamp's basic ingredient —the 3-ring support—you'll have a unique and very special lamp (see Sources of Supply, "Lamp Supplies").

The necessary support consists of 3 brass rings in concentric circles (Fig. 10–8). The rings are supported by rods connected in the center to a brass washer. The largest ring is 11 inches in diameter with 19 equidistant holes spaced around its lower edge; the middle ring is 8 inches in diameter and has 15 holes; the smallest ring is 5 inches in diameter, with 9 holes. From the holes in the brass rings, you hang strings of cooking crystal discs; the center washer is used for attachment of the electrical assembly and light bulb.

If you have a metalworking shop and are pretty handy, you could probably duplicate the 3-ring support in Figure 10–8.

The electrical assembly is sold as a kit or unit (see Sources of Supply). This swag lamp chain kit includes 15 feet of electrical cord, 12 feet of chain, a hanger set, a socket, and a plug. You could also buy the individual parts at your local hardware store.

Fig. 10-8

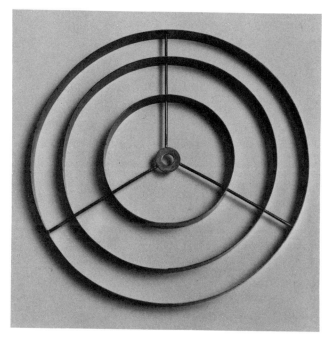

The three-ring lamp support.

My personal preference is to use only 2 or 3 colors to make the discs, varying the patterns: some discs of solid color, others blending 2 or 3 colors, still others with definite designs or patterns in them. All are strung at random.

MATERIALS	EQUIPMENT
cooking crystals	compass
3-ring support fixture	cardboard
swag lamp chain kit	scissors
transparent nylon thread	paintbrush
	2 cookie sheets
	spoon
	aluminum foil
	hot mitts
	metal skewer
	felt tip pen

1. Using the compass, draw 3 circles measuring 1, 1½, and 2 inches in diameter on cardboard. Cut them out to use as patterns.

Cover each cookie sheet with a single length of aluminum foil. Trace circles on the foil with a felt tip pen. Space them at least an inch apart and well away from the edges of the foil. Altogether, you want to make a total of:

> 133 1-inch circles
> 90 1½-inch circles
> 45 2-inch circles

A hanging lamp in progress.

Since it will take quite a while to make 268 discs, you might want to set up a production system whereby you can draw and spoon crystals onto the second cookie sheet while the first one is in the oven. Then you can cool the discs and prepare a new set for baking while the second batch is in the oven.

2. Spoon the crystals ⅛ inch deep into each circle, smoothing the surfaces and the outer edges with your finger or with a small paintbrush.

3. Place the cookie sheet into a 350° oven and bake until the discs are smooth and shiny—about 20 minutes.

4. Cool the discs for approximately 15 minutes; then remove them from the foil.

When all your discs are ready, arrange the 1-inch circles into 19 rows of 7 discs each; the 1½-inch circles into 15 rows of 6 discs each; and the 2-inch circles into 9 rows of 5 each.

5. Wearing the hot mitts, heat the skewer over an open flame and puncture a hole in the top and bottom of all the discs except those which are placed at the bottom of each row. It is necessary to puncture holes only at the top of those discs.

6. Cut 9 lengths of cord, each about 18 inches long. Working from the bottom disc up, string 5 of the 2-inch circles onto each length of cord. Knot the cords as you go to keep each disc firmly in place. Tie the top end of each length of cord through one of the 9 holes in the center brass ring (Fig. 10–9). Cut off the excess cord.

7. Cut 15 lengths of cord about 18 inches each. Working from the bottom disc up, string 6 of the 1½-inch circles onto each length of cord, knotting the cord as you go. Tie the top end of each length of cord through one of the 15 holes in the middle ring and cut off the excess cord (see Fig. 10–9).

8. Cut 19 lengths of cord, each about 18 inches long. Working from the bottom disc up, string seven of the 1-inch circles onto each length of cord, knotting it as you go. Tie the top end of each length of cord through one of the 19 holes in the outer ring and cut off the excess cord (see Fig. 10–9).

9. Attach the electrical assembly through the center washer, following the instructions that come with the kit. Attach the fixture to the ceiling, screw in the light bulb and, at last, the light at the end of the tunnel!

CHAPTER 11

Room Dividers and Panels

COOKING crystals, as an architectural or designer's material, offers real as well as visual division of space without closing it in. Because a finished piece is transparent, light is allowed to pass through it from either side.

When you first begin to think of making a room divider, screen, or window curtain, measure the total amount of space within which you will be working. If the area is large (for example, a space three or four feet wide, spanning floor to ceiling between living and dining rooms), think big! Bright colors, bold designs, and sturdy construction are much more effective than small units filled with tiny details that cannot be seen unless you are right up close. Use nothing smaller than pizza or jelly roll pans. Also, think of the project as a long term endeavor that will take at least a month or two to complete.

If the area is small—for example, the space between a kitchen counter and an overhanging cabinet—you can effectively use smaller cake and pie pans as your molds.

Make sure that all the pans you use for this project are new or perfectly clean and unblemished, since you will be using them without aluminum foil. You don't want your plastic panels to pick up and retain any dirt or scratches from used pans, nor do you want to take a chance on using warped pans, thereby distorting the plastic.

You must also give consideration to the support of the finished divider. How you plan this depends on how permanent a piece you want and how much you can attach to the structure of the house or apartment without irreparable damage when or if the divider is removed.

Any of the following suggestions are possibilities, but in no way represent the only methods of securing the divider in place. You can build a four-sided wooden or stainless steel frame; nail or glue a strip of wood on the ceiling or under the cabinet from which to suspend the parts of the divider with screw eyes; you can nail an additional strip of wood on the floor or counter top for support from the bottom as well as the top. You might be able to work out an attractive arrangement with cafe curtain rods or towel racks, suspending them from either the ceiling or the wall; you can buy spring suspension rods, which require no installation if used in front of a window, but are not terribly strong; or you can use ordinary dowels or curtain rods.

Do not feel that you must use up all the existing space with the plastic pieces; sometimes an airier look is quite effective. For example, if the floor to ceiling height is 7'6" and you are using a 12 inch round pizza pan as the mold, you can fit in 7 vertical circles and use the remaining space for hooks to join one circle to the next. Or you might use just 6 circles and add approximately two inches of chain between each.

You also have choices in attaching one piece to the next. Holes can be made in the baked plastic pieces by piercing them with a heated ice pick. If you place metal eyelets or grommets in the *unbaked* granules, they become permanently embedded in the baked plastic (Fig. 11–1). Large jump rings or brass hoops can be slipped through the holes in the center of the eyelets for attachment. If baked crystals block the hole in the center of an eyelet, the hole can be cleared out with the aid of a heated skewer.

You can buy S-shaped hooks for attaching pieces vertically: they come in a variety of sizes at any hardware store. The hooks are sturdy enough not to bend under the weight of the hanging pieces. The upper curve of the S slips into the bottom hole of one piece, while the lower curve goes through the top hole of the piece below it (see Fig. 11–1).

Fig. 11–1

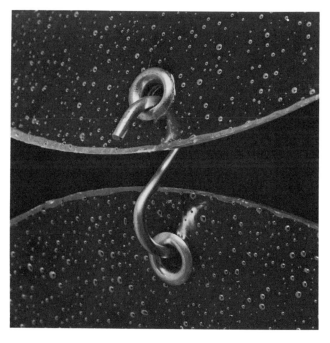

An S hook is used to connect discs through metal grommets.

You can run hardware chain from one piece to another both vertically and horizontally; or, you can attach panels with nylon cord, leather thongs, or plastic lanyard.

All of the units in the divider do not have to be the same shape or size. For example, you can alternate squares and circles or you might use a sequence of one large circle, then two small ones. When you reverse the order on the next row, the same amount of space is used.

This project affords a unique opportunity to incorporate the aspects of cooking crystal craft that most appeal to you. You can effectively do a whole series of leaded pictures. Embedding, mosaics, and hammering are very compatible in the same design. Color scheme alone can be the basis of your project. The room and its furnishings will be a major factor for consideration; if it has, for instance, an Early American motif, you'll want your room divider to have an antique design. Above all, have fun with it!

MODERN ROOM DIVIDER

The floor to ceiling room divider shown in Figure 11–2 consists of 5 rows of 6 circles hanging from a rod attached to the ceiling. You'll need a total of 30 discs; any embedments you want to use must be added to the list of materials.

MATERIALS	EQUIPMENT
25–30 lbs. of cooking crystals	2 12″ pizza pans
55 metal grommets	hot mitts
30 1½″ S-shaped hooks	pliers
6-ft. cafe rod with brackets	tweezers
5 metal cafe rod rings	brush
5 1″ brass jump rings	

1. Place 2 metal grommets on the surface of the pizza pan so that they are lined up on an imaginary diameter, each an inch away from the edge. These will mark the top and the bottom of the circle (see Fig. 11–1).

2. Cover the bottom of the pizza pan with approximately ¾ to a full pound of cooking crystals. The granules should be ¼-inch to ½-inch thick. Make sure the grommets are embedded in the crystals, nudging the loose granules around them tightly; use tweezers to remove any crystals in the hole.

3. Bake the piece in a 350° oven for about an hour; because of the depth of the granules, a longer baking time is needed. When the plastic is smooth and shiny, remove the pan from the oven and allow it to cool for about 30 minutes before removing the disc from the pan.

Repeating steps 1 through 3, make 29 more discs! Remember that 5 of these panels (for the bottom row) will only need *one grommet* apiece.

4. To assemble the divider, first attach the brackets to the ceiling. Slip the metal cafe rod rings over the rod and fasten the rod onto the brackets.

Fig. 11-2

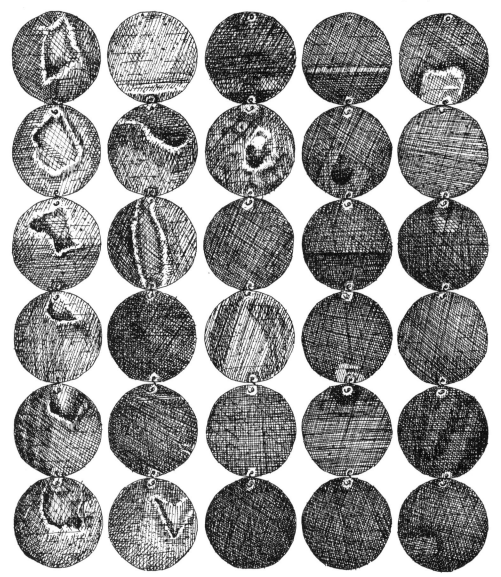

A room divider made from pizza pan molds.

Using pliers, attach a jump ring to each metal ring, and close all the jump rings tightly: these are used to alter the direction in which the hanging discs face.

5. Place the lower curve of the S hook through the top grommet of the first panel and slip the upper curve of the S hook through the jump ring. Attach the second disc to the first, the third to the second, the fourth to the third, and so on, by means of the S-shaped hooks. Remember that the sixth disc has only a top grommet.

Repeat step 5 for the next 4 vertical rows, or until all 30 discs have been attached. Adjust the spacing between the rows and you are finished!

COUNTER TOP PANEL

The divider shown in Figure 11–3 consists of 4 cooking crystal squares joined and soldered together with lead cames. The panel measures 18 by 18 inches and is attached to the underneath of an overhead cabinet, resting on the counter top. You will have to measure the area between cabinet and counter in your kitchen, making appropriate adjustments in the size baking pan you use and the lengths of lead used to join the plastic panels.

MATERIALS	EQUIPMENT
4 lbs. cooking crystals	9″ square baking pan
6-ft. U-channel lead came	soldering iron
3-ft. H-channel lead came	spool of 60/40 solder
4 screw eyes	hot mitts
4 1″ brass rings	pliers
4 metal grommets	right angle or T square
	lead cutter
	newspapers

1. Plan 4 coordinated designs. On each of the 2 designs which are to go at the top of the divider, embed 2 grommets: one at either end, ½″ in from the top and sides (Fig. 11–4).

Working with one panel at a time, fill the pan with crystals, ¼- to ½-inch deep, being careful to surround the grommets with crystals.

2. Bake each of the 4 designs separately in the baking pan until the crystals are smooth and shiny. The length of time will vary, depending on the depth of the crystals and any embedment in your design.

Allow each piece to cool thoroughly before turning it out of the pan.

3. Stretch a 6-foot length of U-channel lead. Bend it to a right angle, with the channel facing inward, on a newspaper covered surface. Use a right angle or T square as a guide and support.

Fit the plastic panel that is to go into the upper left hand corner into the grooves of the lead as shown in Figure 11–4. Leave the remainder of the U came free; you'll use it to surround the other 3 panels as they are added.

4. Cut an 18-inch length of H-channel lead and fit it onto the right vertical side of the first section. Then fit the upper right hand plastic panel into the right angle formed by the H and U lead cames at the top. The left side of this panel is inserted into the H came, with the top and right sides fitting snugly into the U came, as shown in Figure 11–5.

5. Cut 2 lengths of H lead, each 9 inches long; fit the bottom edges of the top panels into these. One length of lead goes on each side, abutting the H came in the center.

Now place the bottom 2 plastic panels in place, fitting the top of each snugly into the H came you just added (see Fig. 11–5).

6. Fit the U-channel lead around the remaining outside edges. When all pieces fit securely and all the angles are straight, solder each joint. Turn the completed sections over and solder the joints on the reverse side for additional support.

7. Line up the 4 screw eyes with the grommets for correct spacing. Screw the eyes into the underside of the cabinet. Open the brass rings and slip each through a grommet in the finished panel, then fasten to the corresponding screw eye. Close the rings and the panel is permanently installed.

Fig. 11-3

A design idea for a four-panel room divider.

Fig. 11-4

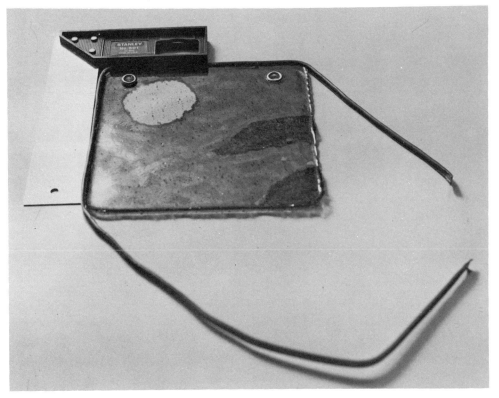

The upper left panel is fitted into the U-shaped lead.

Fig. 11-5

Fitting the sections of the panel together with strips of U and H came.

Sources of Supply

ARTS AND CRAFTS MATERIALS

American Handicrafts
   1011 Foch St.
   Fort Worth, TX 76107
      General craft materials to use in conjunction with cooking crystals

Art & Craft Materials Corp.
   321 Park Ave.
   Baltimore, MD 21201
      General craft materials to use with cooking crystals

Bead Game
   505 N. Fairfax Ave.
   Los Angeles, CA 90036
      Glass, wood, and plastic beads; send 25¢ for catalog

Bergen Arts and Crafts
   Box 381 PC
   Marblehead, MA 01945
      General craft materials; send $1 for catalog, refundable with first order

Economy Handicrafts
   47–11 Frances Lewis Blvd.
   Flushing, NY 11361
      General crafts materials for use with cooking crystals

Glass House Studio
   P.O. Box 3267
   St. Paul, MN 55165
      Transparent suction cups

Holiday Handicrafts, Inc.
   Westhill Rd.
   Winsted, CN 06098
      General crafts materials to use with cooking crystals

Hollywood Fancy Feathers
   512 S. Broadway
   Los Angeles, CA 90013
      Goose feather hackles in colors for embedding

Joli Plastics & Chemical Corp.
   1234 W. 134 St.
   Gardena, CA 90247
      Manufacturer of Crystal Cast® used to set crystals without baking

Malco Distributing Co.
   3825 Industry Ave.
   Lakewood, CA 90712
      Packagers of silica gel used to dry plants and flowers for embedment

Pacific Coast
   745 San Julian
   Los Angeles, CA 90014
      Bamboo shapes to use as frames for cooking crystals

168

COOKING CRYSTALS

Aaron Supply Co.
  Mail Order Dept.
  435 Benefit St.
  Pawtucket, RI 02861

Avalon Industries
  95 Lorimer St.
  Brooklyn, NY 11206
    *Manufacturer of kits containing
      preformed metal frames and
      cooking crystals*

Bergen Arts and Crafts
  Box 381 PC
  Marblehead, MA 01945
    *Crystals available in 5 and 50 lb.
      bags*

Fiber/Glass-Evercoat Co.
  6600 Cornell Road
  Cincinnati, OH 45236

Friends Industries, Inc.
  200 Fifth Ave.
  New York, NY 10010

Hazel Pearson Handicrafts
  4128 Temple City Blvd.
  Rosemead, CA 91770

Lee Wards
  Mail Order Dept.
  1205 St. Charles St.
  Elgin, IL 60120

Quincrafts Corp.
  Mail Order Dept.
  542 E. Squantum St.
  Quincy, MA 02171
    *Cooking crystals or kits combin-
      ing crystals and preformed
      frames*

St. Louis Crafts
  44 Kirkham Industrial St.
  St. Louis, MO 63134

EMBEDMENTS

Bead Game
  505 N. Fairfax Ave.
  Los Angeles, CA 90036
    *Glass, wood, and plastic
      beads for embedment;
      send 25¢ for catalog*

Hollywood Fancy Feathers
  512 S. Broadway
  Los Angeles, CA 90013
    *Goose feather hackles in
      colors for embedment*

Jewelers Emporium
  539 C Northgate Way
  Los Angeles, CA 90027
    *Beads for embedding; send
      25¢ for catalog*

*Many of the suppliers listed under
  Arts and Crafts Materials will
  also carry a variety of objects
  suitable for embedding in
  cooking crystals*

JEWELRY FINDINGS

Jewelers Emporium
  539 Northgate Way
  Los Angeles, CA 90027
    *Jewelry findings and beads;
      send 50¢ for catalog*

Mobob Jewelry Supplies
  125 E. Ninth St.
  Los Angeles, CA 90015
    *Ring findings in which to bake
      cooking crystals*

LAMP SUPPLIES

American Handicrafts
  1011 Foch St.
  Fort Worth, TX 76107
    *Swag Chain Lamp kit; electrical
      assembly for lamp*

Panduro Hobby
  Norrelundves 10
  2730 Herlev, Denmark
    Three-ring brass lamp support

LEAD CAMES

Cadillac Glass
  2212 Pico Blvd.
  Santa Monica, CA 90405

The Stained Glass Club
  P.O. Box 244
  Norwood, NJ 07648

Steven R. Frank Studios
8127 Melrose Ave.
Los Angeles, CA 90046
Whittemore-Durgin
Box 2065 CJ
Hanover, MA 02339

Lead Substitutes

Beagle Manufacturing Co.
4377 N. Baldwin Ave.
El Monte, CA 91731
*Manufacturer of lead shapes
and strips; packaged as
Glaze Glass Craft® kits*
Pactra Industries
6725 W. Sunset Blvd.
Los Angeles, CA 90028
*Manufacturer of Flexi-Lead®;
lead substitute packaged
with Anchor Film®*
Magicraft Div.
Magic American Chemical Corp.
27300 Mercantile Rd.
Cleveland, OH 44122
*Manufacturer of Craft Steel®
liquid lead*

Leadworking Tools

Cadillac Glass
2212 Pico Blvd.
Santa Monica, CA 90405
The Stained Glass Club
P.O. Box 244
Norwood, NJ 07648
Steven R. Frank Studios
8127 Melrose Ave.
Los Angeles, CA 90046
Whittemore-Durgin
Box 2065 CJ
Hanover, MA 02339

Preformed Metal Frames

Aaron Supply Co.
Mail Order Dept.
435 Benefit St.
Pawtucket, RI 02861
*Manufacturer of EZE-FORM®
frames*

Avalon Industries
95 Lorimer St.
Brooklyn, NY 11206
*Manufacturer of kits containing
preformed metal frames and
cooking crystals*
Fiber/Glass-Evercoat Co.
6600 Cornell Road
Cincinnati, OH 45236
*Manufacturer of Bake 'ems®
Metal frames*
Friends Industries, Inc.
200 Fifth Ave.
New York, NY 10010
Hazel Pearson Handicrafts
4128 Temple City Blvd.
Rosemead, CA 91770
Lee Wards
Mail Order Dept.
1205 St. Charles St.
Elgin, IL 60120
Quincrafts Corp.
Mail Order Dept.
542 E. Squantum St.
Quincy, MA 02171
*Manufacturer of Frame-Up®
preformed metal frames*
St. Louis Crafts
44 Kirkham Industrial St.
St. Louis, MO 63134

Special Molds

E. Dehillerin
18–20 Rue Coquilliere
Paris 1er, France
*Fancy petit fours molds: order by
numbers given in Figure 3–4;
send 10¢ apiece, plus postage*
Highly Gifted
418 S. Westgate Ave.
Los Angeles, CA 90049
*Candy molds; an assortment of
12 shapes for $1.25*
Pacific Coast
745 San Julian
Los Angeles, CA 90014
*Bamboo shapes to use as frames
for cooking crystals*

SOLDERING EQUIPMENT

Cadillac Glass
  2212 Pico Blvd.
  Santa Monica, CA 90405
The Stained Glass Club
  P.O. Box 244
  Norwood, NJ 07648

Steven R. Frank Studios
  8127 Melrose Ave.
  Los Angeles, CA 90046
Whittemore-Durgin
  Box 2065 CJ
  Hanover, MA 02339

INDEX

BEATRICE HELLER

I was born and grew up in Lynn, Massachusetts. I was graduated from Lynn Classical High School, attended the University of Massachusetts at Amherst, and was graduated from Boston University with a B.S. in Education in 1953. That same summer, I married and moved to Schenectady, New York. Two years later, my husband and I moved to Los Angeles, California, where we have remained ever since. We have a sixteen-year-old son.

I have worked in public and private schools and have also taught arts and crafts classes to both children and adults.

From 1964 to 1968, I owned and operated a unique school supply and craft center which specialized in innovative materials and methods for use in schools, art classes, camps, and church groups. My partner and I gave lectures, demonstrations, and workshops for children, teachers, and parents wherein we demonstrated materials and techniques; within this framework, we practiced our philosophy of promoting creativity and accepting it in all forms. It was during this period that we first discovered the potential of cooking crystals and I believe that the popularity of this craft in Southern California was due in large part to our efforts. When the business became successful enough to be more demanding of our time than we were willing to give, we sold it.

Since that time, my family has been spending four to eight weeks a year traveling abroad. On a very small scale, I have become an importer of gift items and costume jewelry, discovering exciting or unusual contemporary crafts and jewelry which I bring back to Los Angeles. They are sold to shops on the West Coast through an agent. I have also begun writing for pleasure as well as profit. I attend a series of totally unrelated classes, play too much (yet not enough) duplicate bridge, and am trying to become the world's only Michelin Guide 3-star home!